Drug Discovery

– a pharmacists story

by Ivan Östholm

© 1995 Ivan Östholm, and Swedish Pharmaceutical Press
Swedish Pharmaceutical Press
P.O. Box 1136, S-111 81 Stockholm, Sweden
Tel + 46-(0)8-723 50 00, Fax +46-(0)8-14 95 80
Publisher: Thony Björk
Editor: Ivan Östholm
Translator: George Wood
Swedish title: Från örtavkok till läkemedel
Administration and graphic design: Maud Sundén
Cover: Bennich Information AB, Photos: Ola Husberg, Capsules from Astra AB.
Printed by Kristianstads Boktryckeri AB, Kristianstad 1995
ISBN 91-86274-62-7

Contents

Preface

Patients have asked how their medicines work and how they are created in research laboratories. This book seeks to show them how useful drugs are developed, beginning with discoveries in basic research, followed by industry's goal-oriented research and years of development.

Not only laymen and patients, but also physicians and pharmacologists outside the drug industry, are likely to wonder how their well-documented medicines are created and evaluated. Using examples from the pharmaceutical company Hässle, part of the Astra Group, I aim, in this book, to illustrate how we developed our competence in collaboration with university scientists, and how this cooperation led to the development of some very useful drugs for the treatment of high blood pressure, heart disease and ulcers. These medicines are now used every year by tens of millions of patients in more than sixty countries.

This is the story of how a small Swedish drug company was transformed, thanks to a unique co-operation with university departments and contact with basic research.

The company was founded in 1904. 50 years later, in 1954, when we moved from a small town in southern Sweden to the university city of Gothenburg, sales of the products we had developed amounted to around USD 650,000 a year.

The total sales of the products developed through close collaboration with researchers at the faculty of Pharmacy at the University of Uppsala and at the Faculty of Medicine at the University of Gothenburg had exceeded in 1994 two and a half billion dollars, a significant portion of those sales in the United States.

The collaboration described in this book between the research and development department of an industrial corporation and university researchers ought to be of interest to companies outside the pharmaceutical sector. It is my hope that this example of co-operation between business and university can stimulate other industries to stay in touch with basic research and, in so doing, create new and unique products.

The most important prerequisites for successful collaboration between university and industry are:
– collaboration should be beneficial to both parties.
– shared interest: long-lasting collaboration cannot be built upon economic dependence.
– recognized competence on both sides and mutual respect.
– open collaboration, free of commercial and academic restrictions. Scientists must be able to count on the support and encouragement of their respective organizations.

I've used research reports, minutes of meetings and other notes from the years 1954-1983 as the basis for the descriptions of the projects I initiated as Research Director at Hässle. A number of interviews with scientists and physicians during the years before the Swedish edition of this book was published in 1991 have helped me illustrate developments during this period.

In the final chapter I have tried to summarize what I've learned from both successes and failures. The contact I have had with companies outside the pharmaceutical sector, through lectures and as a consultant have convinced me that the prerequisites for success in research and product development are the same in every field.

Some chapters in the Swedish edition of the book, which were of more interest to a Swedish audience, have been left out of this edition.

In the Swedish edition I thanked scientists at universities, and scientists and other collegues at Hässle, now Astra Hässle, who made it possible to discover and develop the drugs mentioned in the book.

I also thanked all those I interviewed and those who gave me valuable advice how to treat the material and write the book. I shall not repeat those thanks here. They were indeed heartfelt and still remain so.

In this English edition I want to express my gratitude to the translator George Wood and to Maud Sundén. Without her professional work as administrator and graphic designer there never would have been a book. I would also like to thank Gösta Magnusson for his valuable advice and corrections of the manuscript.

I am especially grateful for the grants I have received from
– The Royal Society of Arts and Sciences in Gothenburg.
– Jan Wallanders och Tom Hedelius' stiftelse för samhällsvetenskaplig forskning, Svenska Handelsbankens forskningsstiftelser.

Gothenburg, July 1994

Ivan Östholm

I. Mankind's Search for Cures

Mankind has, since the beginning of time, sought cures for illness and relief from pain, but the means of reaching that goal have varied.

Sacrifices to wrathful gods were thought to be effective when mankind saw suffering as their punishment.

The incantations of medicine men and wizards were tried when sickness and sudden death were attributed to the work of evil powers.

For thousands of years, mankind has searched for remedies in nature. Herbs, animal organs, and minerals have been tried. Thousands of herbs and other parts of plants have been used in decoctions and extracts. Some have been regarded as miracle medicines.

The root of the Ginseng plant has been considered a wonder drug in China for more than a thousand years. Since the Second World War, extracts of this root from Manchuria, Korea, and Japan have become more and more popular in Europe as well. Preparations based on Ginseng or the closely-related Russian Root are said to have a miraculous effect on aches and pains of all kinds, and relieve fatigue as well.

A few hundred years ago Mandrake root was a universal remedy in many European countries. Growing in the Mediterranean region, Mandrake was not only believed to be a cure for sickness, but also to bestow happiness and success.

The alchemists of the Middle Ages tried to influence chemical experiments with incantations and magic rites. They sought "the Philosopher's Stone", which would make it possible to turn base substances into gold. With "the Great Elixir" or "the Elixir of Life", the alchemists hoped to give themselves eternal wellbeing. From the experiments of the alchemists grew true chemical knowledge. Beginning in the 16th and 17th centuries, physicians began to use chemical substances as medications. Drastically acting laxatives and other powerful chemicals probably did more harm than good.

At the beginning of the 19th century there was a reaction to the strong chemical remedies physicians often used. The German physician Hahnemann founded homeopathy. He thought that an illness could be cured with extremely small doses of substances that in high doses caused the same symptoms in healthy people as the disease. He claimed that a substance's effect was strengthened the more it was diluted, thanks to the mystical forces that were conveyed by the dilution process, and the shaking that accompanied each dilution.

It is not just witch doctors, homeopaths, and laymen who have based their remedies on tradition and faith instead of knowledge. Up until this century even physicians educated in medical science often lacked a real understanding of the effect of medicines and how most illnesses should be treated. Even the best educated physicians stuck to methods of treatment that have later been shown to have caused more harm than good.

Bloodletting

One of the most remarkable methods of treatment within conventional medicine was excessive bloodletting to treat pneumonia and other fever diseases. In many cases, when the physicians were not satisfied with drawing blood from their patients by bloodletting, they also applied leeches to their patients' backs to suck blood. A French doctor reported in 1835 that he had compared groups with and without bloodletting. He could demonstrate that bloodletting caused more harm than good. It may be worth mentioning that at that time physicians in France used 30 million leeches a year. Colleagues refused to believe the report on the harmful effects of bloodletting and the physician who wrote it was the object of ridicule for daring to question the doctrines of conventional medicine.

It was to take fifteen more years before doubts were first expressed about the effectiveness of bloodletting and leeches in the treatment of pneumonia. But it wasn't until the end of the 19th century that the me-

The human like appearance of the Mandrake root was seen as a sign of the root's ability to cure human ailments. Mandrake was thought to have the healing power if a dog pulled it up with a string. Illustration from B. Holmstedt and G. Liljestrand, "Readings in Pharmacology", Pergamom Press, 1963.

dical establishment completely condemned the practice of bloodletting for this purpose.

The fact that the medications and cures of both doctors and laymen were almost entirely based on folklore instead of science for hundreds of years steamed from a lack of real knowledge about how a healthy body functions and how it is affected by illness.

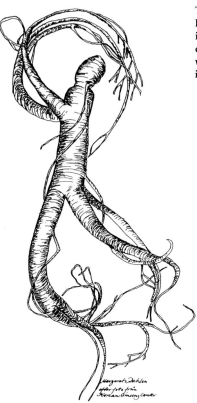

The Ginseng (Panax Ginseng) root has long been thought to have a stimulating and refreshing effect. Like Mandrake, it was sometimes portrayed with a human like appearance. Drawing: Margareta Dahlin.

The knowledge which the pioneers of biological and medical research have given us in the past two or three centuries has completely changed our understanding of how sickness arises and how it can be treated. During the last fifty years the fruits of the work of these great scientists could be harvested in the form of valuable medicines.

A study of the great number of effective and well-documented medicines that have been created during the past half century reveals that progress has been greater and more revolutionary than during any other period of human development.

The methods used to demonstrate the effects of drugs and to establish the risk of their side effects were first developed around forty years ago.

12

II. A Period of Transition

The first two decades after the Second World War represented a true period of transition within healthcare, something that greatly affected the pharmaceutical industry.

The basic research carried out by the departments of physiology, pharmacology and biochemistry at different universities created completely new opportunities for rational pharmaceutical research. It was now possible to develop effective drugs with known mechanisms.

Fifty years ago, knowledge of how drugs should be tested and how their effectiveness could be measured was largely lacking. New sciences, such as bioanalytical chemistry and clinical pharmacology, made it possible to use objective methods to determine the value of a drug for treating a particular disease. By developing methods to determine the amount of active substances in the blood, it became possible to understand the relation between dose and effect in a completely new way.

When the active mechanisms of new drugs were successfully clarified, researchers and clinicians were better able to predict the risk of side effects. In this way, treatment with drugs during the past twenty years has become both safer and more effective.

During the period before and after the Second World War product development and marketing within the Swedish pharmaceutical industry had largely been the responsibility of chemical engineers and economists.

The pharmacists and physicians who were employed within the pharmaceutical industry in the late 50's and 60's didn't just bring with them new knowledge of medicines and their use, they also placed new demands on their companies' goals.

During the 50's and 60's the struggle between old and new ways of thinking was sometimes bitter. The young pharmacists and physicians who became pioneers within the industry often found it difficult to implement the new demands for the value and quality of drugs that they believed to be self-evident be demonstrated.

The decades following the Second World War were a period of transition in another regard as well. As late as the 1950's, women had only subordinate positions in the industry. Major projects today require the participation of fifty to one hundred researchers and technicians. It has been my experience that this collaboration works better when both men and women are involved.

The Doctors Were Powerless

Herbal Decoctions and Poisoned Arrows

When I began as a trainee at a pharmacy laboratory in Stockholm in April, 1938, I was fascinated by the medicines that were made there. In the back of the store was the dispensary with desks where pharmacists stood and prepared medicines from physicians' prescriptions.

Prescriptions for pills were made up several times a day. The pharmacists weighed the active substances on a little scale which was held in the left hand. Often the prescription indicated that one hundred

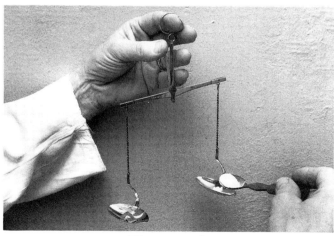

Dispensary scale

15

Doktor HILDING ANDERSSON

Hälsovägen 5 - HÄLSINGBORG

Mottagning vardagar 10—13.
Månd., onsd. och fredagar även 18—19.
Sön- och helgdagar 10—11.
Telefon 6486

Apoteket Björnen
17 AUG. 1939
Hälsingborg
Rec.

Tab. digital.   3.0

Thealalein.   6.0

[illegible]   4.0

[illegible]

D: 1 [illegible] på morgon

2 " " kvällen

5 dagar i veckan

L. *[illegible]*   150

D: 1 [illegible]

[illegible]

Hbg 17/8 39

[signature]

15
20
40 5
20
50
50
00
60

250
28
2.78

120
20
60

150

Ord. för:
1.65

Medtag receptet vid förnyat besök.

[signature] M. Werner

16

pills should be made out of a specified amount of ingredients. After the pharmacist mixed the different substances with lactose or some other inert substance, a trainee added the softener that made it possible to make pills. Fifty pills could be made at a time on a metal table with fifty parallel grooves. The pills were rolled, using a special cup-like tool, until they were round. To make the rolling easier, powdered spores of a club moss called lycopodium were sprinkled over the mixture. Making attractive pills of the same size was something of a handicraft. "Pill rolling" is a profession that has disappeared today.

The pharmacists also mixed liquid medications of various kinds, generally cough medicines and stomach remedies.

My job as the youngest trainee was to prepare the herbal extracts that the physicians prescribed. Decoctions involved soaking ground bark or root in water for half an hour, and removing the active ingredients by boiling. Other herbal preparations, called infusions, were made by pouring hot water over ground leaves or herbs in a process similar to making tea. The mixture was heated for a few minutes, then allowed to cool. Both decoctions and infusions were strained before they were poured into bottles, stoppered with corks and sealed.

The curious student who asked about the healing properties of these herbal remedies seldom received a satisfactory answer.

In this pill prescription, "Fol. digit" means ground leaves from digitalis (Foxglove), "Theocalcin" was a remedy included in the heart medicines of that time. Bromvalerylcarbamid was a sedative. "Massa pil N C" is an instruction to the pharmacist to mix an appropriate paste and make 100 pills.

After the costs for the three active ingredients, comes the cost in öre (100 öre = 1 krona) for the pill paste and the various stages in preparing the pills.

"Liq. tonicus" was a tonic that included arsenic and strychnine.

The pharmacist responsible for preparing this medicine has signed the prescription after the price total.

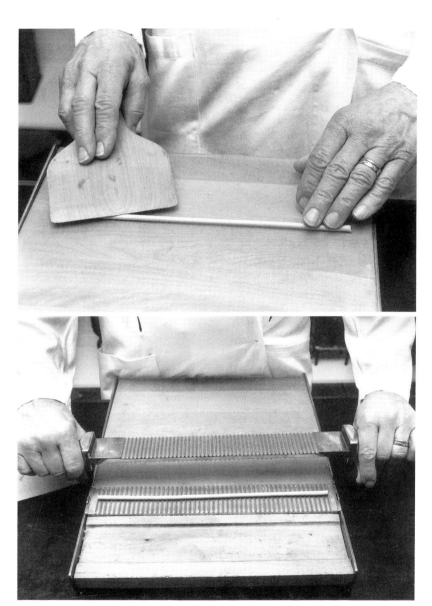

"Pill rolling", a profession that has disappeared.

After the ingredients where mixed in a mortar, where a playing card was often used to help the mixing, the substances needed to make a smooth paste were added. The paste was rolled into an even strand long enough to make fifty pills.

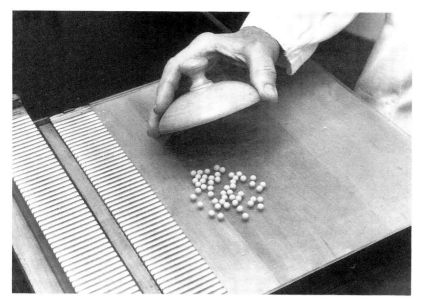

The pills were rolled, using a special tool, until they were round.
(Photos arranged by Roland Ericsson at the Museum at the Swedish Pharmacentical Society)

One common decoction was made from condurango bark. This was prescribed for patients with stomach ailments. When I tried to find out more about its effect and active ingredients, I consulted the manual of "drugs", as the pharmacy's herbal medicines were called. This merely said that condurango bark was imported from South America. The Indians there had discovered that it had a curative effect on stomach ailments. It was even said to have cured stomach cancer, but I couldn't find any evidence for this effect in the scientific literature, so I asked the pharmacist who ran the laboratory:

"Is there any evidence that this bark cures stomach ailments? Does anyone know how it works? The condurango decoction is one of the most common stomach medicines prescribed."

The pharmacist answered with a shrug, "There's certainly no evidence about its effect. Condurango bark is listed in the "Swedish Pharmacopoeia", the book which guides us. The book has been compiled by a number of experts for the Royal Medical Board and sanctioned by the Government. Condurango bark is one of the medications that we are required to stock. Condurango bark is probably often prescribed just because of tradition. The King receives a different decoction from

19

his personal physician for stomach ailments, made from calumba root. That decoction is supposed to give a soothing effect on stomach complaints. But there's no evidence for any effect of that drug in the literature either."

One interesting experience I had during my trainee days was the preparation of an extract of nux vomica, or "semen nucis vomicae" as this herbal drug was called in the pharmacopoeia. Nux vomica comes from a tree in India. The nuts contain strychnine, traditionally used to poison arrows. In Swedish, the poison is called "rävkaka" or "fox cake" in English, probably because it was once used to kill foxes.

While preparing the extract, the pulverized nux vomica nuts were moistened with alcohol. The moistened powder was packed into a brown glass container that narrowed at the bottom, what was called a percolator. Alcohol was poured over the carefully packed powder after which it was allowed to stand for two days before a brown liquid began to drip out at a rate of around twenty drops a minute. When all the liquid was collected, the alcohol was evaporated away. The resulting thick extract was spread out on glass plates and dried, before being ground into powder.

One evening when the pharmacist was on night duty, I was allowed to analyze the nux vomica extract under his supervision. This was an exciting experience and a welcome break from my often monotonous trainee duties. The pharmacy student's day consisted mostly of putting aspirin in small bags, filling capsules with headache powder, and putting all sorts of alcohol-based solutions into bottles. The analysis of the extract was a complicated procedure which took several hours. When it was done, I showed the result to the pharmacist. The level of strychnine had been determined to the tenth of a milligram.

When we had put so much effort into producing and analyzing this medicine, it really seemed that it must be very useful. But when I asked what the extract was used for, and how it worked, the pharmacist really didn't have an answer.

I began to wonder if I had chosen the right profession. I had hoped that the pharmacist would teach me how the medicines worked. I had a hard time believing that an extract prescribed by a doctor for a patient could be something so mystical that no one really knew anything about it. But it was obvious that the use of this nux vomica extract

Percolator. In the upside-down bottle was alcohol which slowly filtered through the drug powder.
(Photo from the Museum at the Swedish Pharmacentical Society)

depended solely on old traditions. I asked again if anyone really knew how the medicine worked?

The pharmacist explained that strychnine was thought to have a restorative effect, but no one knew why. Both strychnine and arsenic were included in medicines that doctors prescribed for patients who complained of fatigue, often as convalescents. Such restorative medicines, or tonics, were included in the Royal Medical Board's compilation of prescriptions for physicians and in the book that pharmacists had to follow when they prepared medicines.

But when I consulted the medical literature, I could find no evidence that either the arrow poison strychnine or arsenic helped patients feel better.

While I was a trainee between 1938 and 1941, I had a strange impression of contemporary medicines. There were few remedies that had a demonstrable effect.

There were some medicines that helped patients live longer. One of these was insulin, which was given to diabetes sufferers, and liver extract, which was prescribed to patients with the blood disease pernicious anaemia. We know today that the latter disease is caused by the body's inability to absorb vitamin B12, which is found in liver extract. Iron deficiency anaemia could be treated by existing iron preparations, but they were far from ideal.

There were pain remedies. The prescription-free aspirin was introduced in 1899. This substance is still included in many tablets for headaches and other ailments. For severe pain, physicians gave morphine. The usual cough medicine was codeine, a weaker derivative of morphine. Sedatives and laxatives were also among the few drugs available then that had a demonstrable effect.

When I read the books that the old pharmacy owner loaned to trainees, they conjured up a picture of a medical world that had, in many ways, stood still for centuries. We used the same plant-based drugs that were sold in apothecaries and market stalls a hundred years before. Much of what was prepared and sold at pharmacies fifty years ago was obviously based on folklore and tradition. True knowledge of the effect and value of different medicines was almost completely lacking.

Among the more unusual remedies we used at the training pharmacy were leeches. These small grey creatures were kept in a glass jar in the cellar. A few times a year some were bought by a customer to suck blood or pus from a boil. According to the instructions in the pharmacopoeia, the leeches should be kept in a container "with drinking water, which should be regularly changed." They never received any food. How they could survive during the months before they sucked blood from a patient is a mystery.

A Medical Revolution

As a pharmacist, I have been amazed at the changes I have seen in the world of medicine during the past fifty years. I turned to Sweden's Royal Physician, Dr. Werner Olsson, an expert in internal medicine, in the Spring of 1988 to get a physician's view of what has happened. I asked him what he remembered about practising medicine in the late 30's and early 40's:

"There were many times when we doctors felt completely helpless when there was nothing we could give a patient. I was an assistant physician at two Stockholm hospitals in the late 30's. We had the best education available at the time, but that was of little help as there weren't any effective medicines to give seriously ill patients.

"If a patient came into the hospital with double pneumonia, all we could do was wait out the crisis, and hope the patient would survive. I remember the feeling the first time we saw the effect of sulfa drugs on a pneumonia patient. New draftees joined the Navy each January, and the following month we almost always had a few cases of pneumonia. But there was no real treatment for those cases. One year, one of my colleagues at the Naval Hospital had a boy who was in very bad shape. There was almost no chance he would make it. We decided to try sulfa tablets which we'd just received at the hospital. The patient was unconscious and couldn't swallow the tablets. We ground them in a mortar and washed the powder into his stomach through his nose.

"The next morning the patient was eating porridge! It was a wonderful experience to see the effect of a new medicine. A few years later, when penicillin arrived, I had similar experiences. It was wonderful to see patients survive severe high fever crises. Those who weren't around before we had sulfa drugs or penicillin must find it hard to understand what those medical advances meant.

"We doctors were also helpless to fight tubercular meningitis. Our patients died without our being able to do anything. Today there are effective antibiotics which save most sufferers from that terrible disease.

"Consumption or tuberculosis was a terror in the 30's and 40's. There was nothing to treat it. We could give our patients cough medicine, and prescribe rest and nourishing food. Those who could stayed in a sanatorium. Higher standards of living, better living conditions and better quality food are largely responsible for the virtual elimination of tuberculosis today. Cases are still appearing, but the infection can now effectively be treated.

"Ulcer patients had a hard time fifty years ago. The most serious cases had to undergo operations. The others stayed in clinics, on strict diets. At first they received only watered down cream and biscuits which contained very little nourishment. This was believed to be a cure for the sores. It was only later we learned they should have a balanced diet.

"The patients who had too much hydrochloric acid in their stomachs were treated with belladonna extract and antacids as a neutralizer. Patients often treated themselves with sodium bicarbonate or chalk as there were no useful antacids at that time. You couldn't give patients belladonna extract or pure atropine in large enough quantities to appreciably reduce the level of hydrochloric acid. If you did, they suffered from extremely dry mouths and had trouble with their vision. Today, there are effective medicines that reduce hydrochloric acid production without the irritating side effects."

When Werner mentioned the problem of side effects, I asked: "How do you regard the risk of side effects with modern medicines? There are so many reports of harmful side effects that the public is easily frightened and may not dare take the medicines that their doctors prescribe."

Werner's answer was very interesting: "Many of the effective medicines that we now use may cause undesirable side effects. But you have to measure the risk of side effects in relation to the value of those medicines that can truly help our patients. A patient who receives a modern beta-blocker for high blood pressure may think it is annoying to have cold fingers and toes.

"But when I was an assistant physician, we had practically no effective medicines at all to give patients with high blood pressure. We tried tranquilizers. First phenemal, later pentymal. Patients became drowsy and often dizzy. At best their blood pressure could be reduced a little, but not enough. We were often forced to see these hypertonia patients lying helpless after a stroke. Those were the side effects that worried us when there weren't any effective medicines. Death was the side effect we were most afraid of, when we didn't have antibiotics to use against severe infections."

Among the journals and abstracts I had brought with me, I found a quote from the Nobel laureate Ernst Chain. When he was asked about the value of modern scientific advances, he answered:

"I consider medicines to be one of the greatest blessings of our age... perhaps the greatest. I shudder to think of the torture of having a limb amputated without anaesthesia. I would hate to be in the position we were in before the arsenal of modern medicines and vaccines were available to physicians, when I could helplessly watch my wife die of childbed fever, see my friends broken by tuberculosis, or my children lamed by polio."

Werner admitted: "That's a true picture of what we are spared today... Imagine how helpless we were when faced with a leukaemia patient. Today many can be cured. Others can live for several years.

"Don't forget how much more difficult it was for doctors to make diagnoses fifty years ago. We didn't have access to the diagnostic methods that doctors today regard as a matter of course. I'm thinking of the help we now get from specialities where research and modern technology have completely revolutionized diagnostics."

Transplantation Surgery Got Banner Headlines

Modern medicines have given specialists in internal medicine previously unimagined ways to save lives and give relief to their patients. The most dramatic breakthroughs, however, concern surgeons and organ transplant operations.

The following description of some of the milestones in this field have come from Yngve Edlund, Professor Emeritus of Surgery at the University of Gothenburg:

When the South African surgeon Christian Barnard reported in 1967 that his surgical team had carried out a heart transplant, it was first page news all over the world. However, that wasn't the first organ transplant operation. As early as 1954 the first kidney transplants were carried out in Boston. Today, more than 200,000 kidney transplants have been performed around the world.

Since the first heart transplants were carried out in 1967 and 1968, thousands of patients have received new hearts. The liver and pancreas are two other organs that can be replaced today. Bone marrow transplants have saved countless children suffering from leukaemia.

A number of drugs that have been developed by the pharmaceutical industry has made it possible for surgeons to transplant organs:

– Penicillin and other antibiotics have reduced the risk of infection in connection with operations.

– Modern anaesthetics such as Halotan, in combination with laughing gas (nitrous oxide), have given surgeons and anaesthetists ways of anaesthetising patients without discomfort.

– Intravenous anaesthetics began to be used during the Second World War.

– When the Swedish pharmaceutical company Astra introduced the local anaesthetic Xylocain (lidocain) in 1948, it happened at a time when anaesthesiology had developed into an independent speciality within medicine. Xylocain was so unique that even after half a century it is still the world's most used local anaesthetic.

– Synthetic variants of the South American arrow poison curare, developed by the pharmaceutical industry as muscle relaxants, have also helped surgeons performing operations.

– Remedies which affect the immune system were developed during the 50's. Use of these drugs became one of the most important tools in transplant surgery since they prevent the rejection of foreign organs.

Psychiatry, a Young Science

The effective medicines that gave internal specialists and surgeons after the Second World War a completely new means of treating their patients had no counterpart in psychiatry. It would be a long time before doctors at mental hospitals experienced the same revolutionary improvements as their colleagues. In February 1988, I asked Björn-Erik Roos, then Professor of Psychiatry at the University of Uppsala, why this was so?

Björn-Erik Roos described the situation within psychiatry:

"The medicines that were developed by the pharmaceutical industry's researchers after the Second World War rested on basic research that had been carried out at the end of the last century and the first half of the Twentieth Century. It was the knowledge of how the heart and blood vessels worked that made it possible to start goal-oriented research projects within the pharmaceutical industry to develop medicines that reduced blood pressure and remedies for the treatment of heart disease. That's how you worked at Hässle. Understanding of how biochemical mechanisms controlled other organs made it possible to create effective drugs that affected those organs. One interesting example is your Ulcer Project at Hässle which led to the drug omeprazol (known as Losec®, Prilosec®) for the treatment of gastric ulcers.

"The brain is the most complicated organ in the human body. Our knowledge of the brain's functions has been, and still is, far too incomplete. That is why it has taken much longer to develop effective drugs within psychiatry.

"When I lecture on psychiatry, I usually don't talk about mental illness. Instead I emphasize that the symptoms we see have their roots in changes to the brain. It is only now that we are beginning to understand how to treat these disorders.

"During the 40's and the beginning of the 50's there were practically no medicines to give patients with serious mental symptoms. We had nothing to give people suffering from the severe personality changes we call psychoses. There were no drugs to give patients suffering from depression or severe anxiety.

"The most agitated patients at mental hospitals were calmed with injections of morphine-scopolamine. We also tried opium and strong sedatives. The most violent patients received electric shocks. At the mental hospital where I worked at the beginning of the 50's, the staff said that a patient should be "el-ed". It was a very unpleasant experience.

"At the hospital there was a special room with a solid bed permanently fastened to the floor. Six strong male nurses forced the patient down onto the bed, electrodes were fastened to his head and when the

27

current was turned on, the patient lost consciousness, suffered cramps, and turned blue in the face. When he woke up, the patient was calm and peaceful. The most difficult cases could be "el-ed" several times a week. Then they would be easier to handle for a while.

"The careful electric shocks that are now used with good effect for the treatment of some cases of depression can't be compared to the old treatment "el-ing".

"When chlorpromazine arrived in Sweden in the mid-50's, it was the first time doctors at mental hospitals had a medicine with which they could treat psychoses like schizophrenia. After the introduction of chlorpromazine, patients no longer had to be "el-ed". The French pharmaceutical company Rhone-Poulenc, which created chlorpromazine, has certainly made a major contribution to psychiatry.

"The first effective medicine for the treatment of depression was imipramine, developed by the Swiss pharmaceutical company Geigy.

"What's interesting is that neither chlorpromazine nor imipramine was the result of goal-oriented research intended to find psychiatric medicines. Both drugs were the result of work to develop new remedies for treating allergies.

"Chlorpromazine was interesting for heart surgery, because it had the ability to lower body temperature, which explains the brand name Hibernal, after the way animals lower their body temperature when they hibernate.

"Chlorpromazine's effect on psychoses and imipramine's effect on depression was discovered by doctors when these drugs were used in clinical tests for different purposes.

"Besides giving doctors completely new ways of treating mental patients, chlorpromazine and imipramine became tools in the researchers' hands. They have contributed to clarifying several biochemical mechanisms in the functioning of the brain. Swedish research has significantly contributed to this research field."

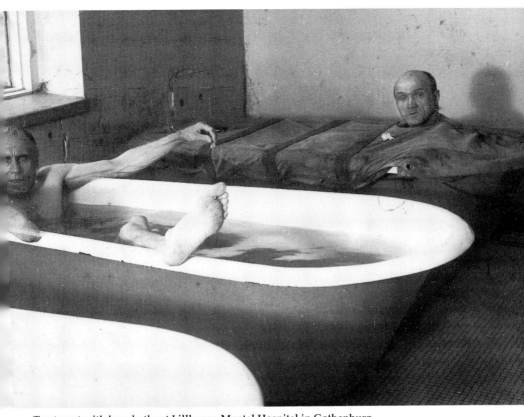

Treatment with long baths at Lillhagen Mental Hospital in Gothenburg.
   Before chlorpromazine and other psychopharmacological drugs existed, long
baths were one of the methods mental hospitals were forced to use to calm violent
patients. *(Photo: Lillhagens Museum, Britta Magnusson)*

III. Forks in the Road and Milestones

As late as the 50's, most Swedish pharmaceutical companies still could not present any achievements based on their own creative research. With a few important exceptions, their products were copies of the old remedies of the physicians' prescriptions or contained drugs that had been copied from the innovations of foreign companies.

In a pamphlet called "New Product Development Within the Swedish Pharmaceutical Industry" (distributed by the Pharmaceutical Industry Association), Inge Ehrlen gave a good picture of the preparations developed by Swedish companies up to the Second World War.

There were useful drugs available, but they had been created by researchers outside the industry. Astra's local anaesthetic Xylocain® (lidocain) was created by chemists at the University of Stockholm, and then developed by Astra into a well-documented medicine.

Pharmacia's blood replacement Dextran was an important original product created by biochemists at the university. Biochemists all over the world are familiar with Pharmacia's Sefadex, which is an aid for separating products within biochemical research and production. This product was developed from Dextran.

Unfortunately, Ferrosan's original products AP and PAS were not patented. Both drugs could have been important export products. AP has had a major application in dissolving blood clots and preventing their formation. PAS was the first drug available to physicians for the treatment of tuberculosis.

The researcher who created these two valuable drugs was Jörgen Lehmann of the Sahlgrenska Hospital in Gothenburg.

31

Hässle was like a large apothecary laboratory during the 50's, more than any other Swedish pharmaceutical company at the time. There was no creative synthesis at work at all.

At that time, no comprehensive documentation was required to demonstrate a preparation's medical value. It was often enough to include a certificate from a doctor who had tested the tablets with the registration application to the National Medical Board.

Even after moving to Gothenburg in 1954, Hässle was supposed to continue producing simple preparations for the Swedish market. My first job was to make cough syrups, ointments, and tablets, using the familiar unpatented remedies. However, my instructions stipulated that I could count on receiving a few new patented substances from the Astra research laboratories. It was believed that the company's new facilities in Södertälje, southwest of Stockholm, would be such a creative and productive environment that the parent company would be unable to utilize everything that was produced. So we at Hässle would be allowed to use some of their findings in our own product development programmes. But pharmaceutical research turned out to be much more difficult than anyone had thought.

One reason for the difficulties in creating new drugs that clearly existed during the 50's and 60's was the lack of pharmacologists and biologists with the competence and desire to work in the pharmaceutical industry.

Astra's research in the late 50's, like Hässle's, followed the same principles that the major foreign drug companies had successfully used since the Second World War. These companies, which were based in Britain, Switzerland, the United States and West Germany had large research and development departments each employing more than a thousand researchers and technicians. Each successful medicine developed in these companies' laboratories was the result of chemists synthesizing thousands of new chemical compounds, followed by tests known as screening.

Following large standard programs, pharmacologists looked for the effects of these chemicals in animal experiments to see if they were worth testing as medicines. Between 5,000 and 8,000 substances could be tested before a useful medicine was found. In many of these pharmaceutical companies it was the chemists who led the research programs.

The problem with this kind of drug research was not just that it demanded huge resources. Unfortunately, the new medicines that were developed were, as far as biological effects were concerned, often just variants of known drugs. Since the testing methods used for the screening process were the same as those used earlier by other research groups, one could hardly expect to achieve any unique discoveries.

Nevertheless, researchers and clinicians occasionally succeeded in finding completely new mechanisms. Unexpected discoveries were made by observant physicians during clinical tests. When researchers at the American pharmaceutical company Merck synthesized and tested new sulfa preparations for treating infections, they also discovered a new principle for treating high blood pressure.

We could never count on having the major resources necessary for success within traditional pharmaceutical research, based on the synthesis and screening of large series of chemical compounds at Astra. We were forced to find other ways. It was Hässle's university contacts in Gothenburg that showed us in which direction we should go.

When Erik Kistner left his position as chairman of Hässle's Board shortly after I began working for the company, it turned out that there was little support at Astra for research. I received clear orders only to work with preparations for the Swedish market under the supervision of the company's President, Tore Norlander.

The budget for the laboratory work that was supposed to provide us with new preparations while at the same time improving the old unmodern remedies, was no larger than USD 40,000. This corresponded to four percent of Hässle's sales, including the products we sold as agents for foreign companies.

A strong desire to start some kind of research drove me to seek help from researchers at the Pharmaceutical Faculty, then at the University of Stockholm, now at the University of Uppsala, and at the Medical Faculty at the University of Gothenburg. The contributions of these scientists were of great importance for Hässle's growth, as well as for the entire Astra Group.

Looking back at Hässle's growth from a company with modest sales of its own products of USD 600,000 in 1954 to an annual turnover of two and a half billion dollars 40 years later, it is clear that something dramatic must have happened to the old company. From its beginning in 1904 until 1954 it was a small operation only selling on the Swedish market. But by the early 90's, exports and foreign sales accounted for more than 90 percent of the two and a half billion dollar turnover.

I am convinced that the foremost reasons for Hässle's success, despite our small resources, were the new directions indicated by our university consultants and our early employment of highly qualified people in our own research and development department. *Earlier than any other pharmaceutical company in Sweden, we were successful in employing physicians specializing in pharmacology, clinical pharmacology, and experimental medicine. We could build up a team working with chemists and pharmacologists in a stimulating common effort to create better medicines for which there were clear needs.*

The gradually changing goals for the company's product development, as well as for the entire enterprise, was of great importance for attracting and keeping qualified researchers.

But when we moved to Gothenburg in 1954 there was no detailed goal definition for the company's activities. It was taken for granted that our goal was to increase profits and sales. Company President, Tore Norlander, was convinced that the way to reach that goal was to develop as many products as possible.

Before the move, Astra's management decided that all products outside of drugs would be transferred to other units within the Group. Hässle would concentrate on developing medicines, but only for the Swedish market.

During the 60's there was an increasingly intensive debate within the company about our future goals. Sven-Arne Norlindh, who aside from his duties as Marketing Director also served as Vice President between 1954 and 1961, at which time he became President, several times expressed the need for higher goals than just producing usable medicines for the Swedish market on more than one occasion. According to minutes from several meetings in the late 50's, even at that early date he was calling on us to concentrate on preparations that met real medical needs. Co-operation with the Swiss company Giegy had shown the value of unique products and skilful marketing.

When Lennart Sölvell, our first physician with Assistant Professor competence, was employed in 1961, the demands for higher goals were intensified. According to minutes from a meeting in 1961, Lennart Sölvell stressed that higher objectives for our product development would mean increased goodwill among doctors. In addition, our own people would be stimulated and motivated to make greater contributions.

In 1971 Kjell Holmquist, who had become President three years before, took the initiative for renewed discussions about the company's long-term objectives. These were established as:

<u>to</u> *create medicines which would contribute to the development of pharmaco-therapy. This meant that drugs we intended to market would, in some way, be better than all other preparations available to physicians.*

34

<u>to</u> demonstrate the value of our drugs through comprehensive documentation of their effects and the risk of side effects.

<u>to</u> provide correct information about the proper use of our products.

In addition, the statement of objectives also said that the company should seek to give all employees meaningful work.

In order to reach these high goals we would strive for high profitability, however, this would not be a goal in itself, but rather be a way to ensure the company's future, as well as procuring the means by which we would reach the lofty objectives upon which we had agreed.

There is no doubt that these objectives were decisive for our ability to employ and keep qualified researchers.

When I had the statement of objectives published in the "Swedish Medical Journal" in the early 70's, it attracted a great deal of interest. It was the first time that a Swedish pharmaceutical company had so clearly declared that it aimed to create and market products that were an improvement over current medical treatments.

FÖRTECKNING

ÖFVER

FARMACEUTISKA PREPARAT

FRAMSTÄLLDA Å

APOTEKETS I HÄSSLEHOLM
KEM. FARM. LABORATORIUM

PROFVER SÄNDAS PÅ BEG. GRATIS OCH FRAKTFRITT

THIOGADOL

Ersätter Ichtyol och Thigenol, af hvilka stora mäng-der importeras hit till Sverige. Thiogadol är fram-ställdt genom sulfonering af en på särskildt sätt fram-ställd svafvelolja, produktens tvättning och öfverföring till ammoniumsalt. Vi kunna garantera, att vår Thio-gadol är fullt lika bra som det utländska preparatet. Thiogadol har med godt resultat profvats först och främst af numera aflidne Prof Magnus Möller samt af en annan framstående hudspecialist i Stockholm, hvars namn vi tyvärr ej äga rätt att nämna, dess-utom af ett flertal andra läkare.

Alla af oss framställda preparat äro betyd-ligt billigare än motsvarande utländska.

Apotekets i Hässleholm
Kem. Farm. Laboratorium

Hässleholm 1912, Norra Skånes Tryckeri

From Folklore to Knowledge

Many surprises awaited me at Hässle. The most shocking was that there were no acceptable analytic methods for monitoring the quality of the company's drugs.

The company's founder, pharmacist Paul G. Nordström, started the company in 1904 as a side-line to his drug store in the southern Swedish city of Hässleholm. As a pharmacist, he had a certificate from the Royal Medical Board allowing him to produce medicines. He also had a royal permit to run a pharmacy. Medicines mixed by pharmacists were always believed to have the proper composition, partly because, in the old days, it was impossible to analyse the medications produced in the pharmacies.

There was no way to test that the remedies produced actually contained the right amount of active ingredients. You were forced to trust that the phamarcists followed the instructions in the relevant pharmacopoeia.

The first legal norm for the production of medicines in Sweden was laid-down in the pharmacopoeia of 1686. The 11th edition of the pharmacopoeia, which came out in 1946, certainly required modern analytic methods to be used to test most medicines, but pharmacies lacked the resources to apply them. In most cases, pharmacists were forced to rely on exactly following the instructions of the pharmacopoeia.

One of the first drug catalogs in Sweden was Paul Nordström's from 1912.

37

The equipment at Hässle's laboratories was very simple in 1955. As the only qualified pharmacist I had to carry out the tests which required pharmaceutical competence.

To help pharmacists meet the responsibility of testing medicines, the Pharmaceutical Control Laboratory (AKL) was founded in 1923, responsible for developing test methods and for testing samples of the medicines sold by pharmacies.

In the beginning, the AKL's primary function was to monitor the industrially manufactured preparations sold by pharmacies. When the Swedish state introduced controls on all industrially manufactured medicines in 1934, the AKL changed its orientation to helping pharmacies control the medicines they produced themselves. Beginning in 1946, the AKL carried out tests of all raw ingredients bought by pharmacies. Because of the activities of the AKL, Swedish pharmacies held a rather unique position in the world.

Alongside his pharmacy, Paul Nordström founded an independent operation producing medicines. He was one of the pioneers of the Swedish pharmaceutical industry. At the respectable age of fifty plus he went to Germany to learn how to make tablets and sugar-coated pills. From what I could discover, Nordström developed and applied the testing methods for factory manufactured preparations that were possible with the scientific knowledge of the 30's and 40's.

During the 50's, improved analytic testing of the industrial production of Hässle's preparations was obviously necessary. We had to be sure that the right ingredients in the right amounts were present in our preparations before they were allowed to leave the factory. There was an urgent need for us to develop analytic tests as soon as possible for all our products.

When I took up this problem with our President in the Fall of 1954, there was little interest in allocating resources for developing testing methods. He didn't think this was productive work. Instead, he wanted to see new products quickly developed.

I contacted Göran Schill, at that time associate professor of Analytic Chemistry at the University of Stockholm, and later Professor at the Pharmaceutical Faculty at the University of Uppsala. He understood my situation, and the analytic methods he worked out made it possible for us to continue to manufacture the products we needed to survive and develop.

The work carried out by skilled researchers at Göran Schill's department made it possible for us, after a few years, to develop the analytical methods we needed for testing the company's new products. Later we developed further techniques sensitive enough to allow us to study what happens when a drug is ingested into the human body.

The substances formed by transformation in the liver, the so-called metabolites, could also be measured with the separation and analytical methods made available to us by Göran Schill's department. Our ability to study the relation between a given dose of a drug, subsequent levels of that drug in the blood, and its therapeutic effect, was an important factor in Hässle becoming one of the leading pharmaceutical companies.

This understanding of bioanalytical chemistry and the new science of clinical pharmacology gave us a lead over many competitors. It was this competence that made it possible to gain the approval of the American FDA for the drug metoprolol (Lopressor® and Toprol-XL®) in 1978, without a single clinical study having been carried out in the United States, something that had never happened before and has not happened since. But it took us a long time to get that far.

When I appealed to Göran Schill in the Fall of 1954 for help in developing a testing method for the preparation I most felt needed modern analytical control methods, Spasmolysin, he was sceptical:

"It's not easy. There are no existing methods for separating the preparation's five active ingredients from each other and determining the amount of each in the tablets. I'll have to find a way. The big problem is that I don't have an assistant. My time is taken up by 100 teaching hours this year and supervising my students' laboratory work four days a week."

He struggled with the problem for several months, often late at night. One discovery led to Göran's doctoral dissertation. That discovery turned out to be of great importance for the research at his department. In a letter to me in June 1981 he described the sudden insight that is characteristic of important discoveries:

"The memory of it is still strong. It must have been in the Fall of 1954. I was in the Associate Professor's room on the second floor of the Chemistry Department. The most difficult part of the problem was to measure the drug methylhomatropin which was present in the tablets in very small amounts.

"There were no reasonable methods in the literature. The only method that was described said you should add a reagent that caused a precipitation when it came in contact with methylhomatropin. The precipitation was supposed. to be collected in a filter, dried and weighed. I have always disliked these methods where you measure very small amounts by weighing. It's very easy to make a mistake. So I was trying to find another way.

"Instead of collecting the precipitation in a filter, I added chloroform to the mixture. When I shook the mixture, I could see that the chloroform had taken a deep yellow color. Some new substance must have dissolved into the chloroform. When I shook the chloroform with just the reagent, it didn't turn yellow. I suddenly got the idea that the reagent could have bonded to the methylhomatropin in what is called an ion-pair. The two molecules had, hand-in-hand you might say, created a yellow-colored substance, that dissolved in the chloroform.

40

"Neither before nor after have I felt so strongly that I've made an important discovery and realized its potential."

Göran Schill ended his letter:

"The work with Hässle was then, as ever since, of very great importance for me. It brought with it new and important problems to be solved."

This was the first time, but certainly not the last, that I realized that university scientists can be stimulated into important contributions by appealing for their help in solving problems so difficult that they are perceived as challenges.

Now afterwards, however, I think it is remarkable that Göran Schill took it upon himself to help me with a number of difficult analytical techniques without any promise of economic compensation. I had been forced to tell him:

"I have no money. The laboratory budget is so small I can't pay you anything this year. Perhaps not next year either. My request to employ a chemical engineer to develop analytical techniques was turned down. Group management prefers to see better profitability and increased contributions from Hässle. It's getting difficult to get resources to develop new medicines. Many of the old remedies are so deficient that all of our resources are going towards improving them."

Thanks to Göran Schill's work over a period of several years, we could solve the most pressing analysis problems. When, in the early 60's, the company began a rapid expansion, we were able to compensate Göran Schill for his contributions during our development phase by supporting research at his department.

The analytic tests and modern analysis equipment for pharmaceutical substances were not needed solely for testing if our products contained the right active ingredients in the right amounts. What the company management seemed to have difficulty understanding during the 50's was that qualified analytical techniques are some of the most important tools of pharmaceutical research in gaining the knowledge needed to initiate and carry out projects.

It was only when the biologists and medical researchers gained access to sensitive analytical techniques that they found new ways to answer questions that previously had been considered impossible to solve. Thanks to the refined analysis systems that were developed during the 60's and 70's, we could better determine the relationships between the doses that were given to patients and the level of active substances in the blood, as well as the intended effect of the medical treatment. During those years we succeeded in moving from folklore, often fumbling in the dark, to a real knowledge of the effect and value of our medicines.

Even where simpler preparations were concerned, it was more and more necessary to learn about their effects and document their value. The first remedy we tried to document was the soluble aspirin Bamyl. I developed it in the Fall of 1954.

I published a study, together with my colleague Tord Lagerwall, in which we indicated the factors that affected the solubility of the aspirin in Bamyl.

I remember the commotion caused by this simple publication. One day I was called in to the company President's office. Deeply serious, he read a letter from the Group management. I was guilty of serious misconduct. Company secrets had been published in such a way that competitors could take advantage of them. This was not to be repeated. Today we think it obvious that a medicine's qualities be publicised, along with the studies that have established the advantages of the medicine over previously existing remedies. I believe such openness is a prerequisite for work with university researchers.

Several times I realized that the time was not yet right for open collaboration between the pharmaceutical industry and university scientists. The door had been closed from both sides. Industry, because they were afraid that know-how would leak to competitors, while the university researchers felt that they would sully themselves if they worked with profit-making companies. They were also afraid that industry would influence free and open research.

The work with Göran Schill was Hässle's first worthwhile contact with university scientists. The difficult analytical problem that he was asked to solve in 1954 was the beginning of a collaboration that continued for several decades, and which has been of major importance for Hässle's growth.

The man responsible for the next step, opening the doors of the Medical Department at the University of Gothenburg, was Björn Folkow.

The University Doors Opened

The week before Christmas 1954 I met Björn Folkow for the first time. He was then associate professor at the Department of Physiology, University of Gothenburg, where several years later he became Chairman of the department.

I presented a proposal of our first research project and asked for help with tests on animals. The goal of the project was a new kind of tablet with a timed effect. The active drug would be slowly released from the tablets. In my eagerness to "sell the idea" I may have been too pushy. Björn interrupted:

"That's no problem. I can probably help you with the animal tests you need. The project is interesting. It must be a major medical priority to develop tablets that patients can take in the morning and in the evening instead of three or four times a day. As you say, you may also be able to reduce the risk of side effects when the whole amount of a drug is not released at once as with an ordinary tablet. I'd be happy to help you on."

We discussed the design of the experiment and the preliminary studies we had made to try to develop the desired tablets. Finally I had to admit the painful truth:

"The problem is that I don't have any money in my laboratory budget to pay for the experiments. And it looks like there won't be any more money next year either for this kind of research."

Björn must have thought that I looked worried. "That's really not a problem," he said. "When I've finished my own experiments on circulation in cats, I can continue with your experiments. I can put a tablet in a sleeping cat's small intestine and record the effect of the physiologically active compounds we decide to use. If we use an ordinary tablet the first time and then test tablets with different time releases later, we can learn how the tablets should be made for the appropriate time release of a drug."

The experiments Björn Folkow helped us to perform in 1955 made it possible for us to apply for a patent and to test the new kind of tablets, which were called Durules.

Björn Folkow was my first contact with the Medical Faculty at Gothenburg University. It wasn't easy for an unknown pharmacist at the little pharmaceutical company Hässle to establish contact with a university researcher in the 1950's. Björn helped me in my contacts with other departments at the university.

Hässle was even less known abroad. It was hard to make academic contacts. When I talked to a pharmacologist in Chicago in 1962, he couldn't even find Gothenburg on a world map. Finally his face lit up and he exclaimed, "Oh, you're from Folkow's place!"

When he understood that we were working with the well-known physiologist, we were accepted.

In Sweden, it wasn't easy for the pharmaceutical industry to find academic partners in the 50's and 60's. The not uncommon tabloid headline "Industrialist Buys Professors" illustrates the negative attitude of the media to co-operation between university researchers and industry.

The help Björn Folkow provided by working with us at an early stage and opening doors to contacts with other university departments were later important arguments when the government and parliament discussed a proposal to create part-time positions at universities for researchers from industry. After these positions, called adjunct professors, were introduced in 1973 the criticism of this co-operation ended. The tabloid article I quoted above referred to my letter to the University of Gothenburg concerning the proposal.

There has been interest abroad in the kind of co-operation between academia and industry that we developed in Gothenburg. In "Decision Making in Drug Research", published in 1983, Franz Gross described the work between Hässle and university researchers as "... a Swedish model... worth copying."

As a member of the science council which we started in 1957, the so-called Consultant Conferences, Björn Folkow was responsible for many important contributions to Hässle's research. His experience in his own field, the physiology of the circulatory system and the nervous system, contributed to many projects, especially those aimed at developing medicines to fight heart disease and for the treatment of high blood pressure. He gave us advice and support when we got stuck while working on the project that led to alprenolol and metoprolol (Lopressor and Toprol-XL). At one point he also saved the ulcer medicine project which gave us omeprazol (Losec, Prilosec).

The project that led to the drug felodipin (Plendil) in 1988 rested largely on discoveries made at Björn Folkow's department. In minutes dated October 1960, it was noted that Björn Folkow had suggested that we start a project with the goal of developing a medicine to reduce blood pressure by dilating peripheral blood vessels.

The project was deemed to be important, and it was decided that Hässle would begin work on it as soon as the necessary resources were available. For several years we tried to find funds for the project.

Unfortunately it was 15 years before we could realize our plans to develop a new medicine for the treatment of high blood pressure.

During the years that we waited for resources for the project, Björn Folkow often spoke about how urgent it was to develop a drug that would dilate the peripheral blood vessels so the heart could pump blood with less resistance. He underlined that such a medicine would be ideal for the treatment of high blood pressure, especially in those cases where other drugs had proved ineffective. But it wasn't until 1975 that we were able to employ the staff needed to build up a research project based on these ideas.

It started in the Spring of 1975 with a telephone from Björn.

"Can you find a job for one of our younger researchers? We don't have a position at the department he can support his family on. Bengt Ljung is such a capable researcher that it would be a shame for him to leave his research for clinical work just to earn a decent income."

Björn sounded upset when he went on:

"It's really tragic that the government doesn't understand how important it is to concentrate on basic research. Nowadays the priority is for goal-oriented research, development projects, and what they call societal-oriented research. Whatever that is… as if there was societal-alienated research."

He was disappointed that there was no position at his department for one of their best scientists. Bengt Ljung studied the physiology of the blood vessel musculature with Björn's close colleague Börje Johansson, who also took part in our consultant conferences and who was later employed by Hässle.

Bengt Åblad, who was then head of our pharmacology department, contacted Bengt Ljung.

Since Bengt Ljung planned to go into clinical work, and because he was hesitant to work for industry, we agreed to try a somewhat unusual solution. Bengt Ljung, who was an assistant professor in Physiology, began working at Hässle's Pharmacological laboratory one day a week. The idea was for him to spent a year getting the feel of the place. Would a scientist working solely on basic research feel comfortable within a goal-oriented industrial project?

When we discussed the objective of Bengt Ljung's work with Hässle, we decided that he should work on a project to develop a better drug to reduce blood pressure than was already available. The idea was that the new drug would reduce blood pressure through a different mechanism than that used by our beta-blockers, alprenolol and metoprolol. By continuing to work at Björn Folkow's department and maintaining contact with his colleagues there, we believed Bengt Ljung would be in a good position to succeed.

After a few months Bengt was so interested in the project's aims that he began to work full-time at Hässle. However, he maintained close contacts with his university colleagues.

During his first year Bengt Ljung developed a completely new screening method for testing the substances that the chemists developed. Using a device built at Hässle's experimental workshop, he developed a research model where the effect of the blood pressure reduction of various substances were studied on rats with high blood pressure.

By 1977 we synthesized the substance H154/82, which proved to have such a good effect in reducing blood pressure that we decided to go on to tests on human subjects, hopefully followed by clinical tests.

Our clinical pharmacologist Gillis Johansson led the clinical tests on H154/82. I still remember how Gillis, who usually expresses himself quietly and carefully, enthusiastically reported on the extraordinarily positive reductions in blood pressure he had observed since the first patient studies with the drug had been conducted.

For twelve years, Bengt Ljung led the project from the first idea to the final drug felodipin (H154/82), which under the name Plendil® was approved in 1988 by the authorities in Sweden and several other countries.

Plendil reduces blood pressure by working directly on the muscle cells of small blood vessels so that they relax allowing them to dilate.

The blood pressure drops, and the work of the heart is eased, when it can pump against lower resistance. The biological principle that Plendil represents is called calcium-blockade. There are other drugs that use the same principle which also expand the arteries so that blood pressure is reduced, but they also have an undesirable effect on the heart muscle. Removing this effect was one of the goals of our project. That we achieved this to a great extent makes Plendil a very valuable medicine for the treatment of hypertension. Plendil is active against all degrees of high blood pressure. In those cases where patients need to be treated with more than one drug, Plendil works well in combination with the beta-blocker metoprolol.

When the patent application for this group of blood pressure reducing substances was filed in June 1978, our chemists had synthesized 500 new substances, the biological properties of which were being studied by pharmacologists.

The active drug in Plendil was so difficult to work with and make into tablets with a twenty-four hour timed release effect, that five years' work by more than twenty scientists and technicians was required to solve the problems.

When Plendil was presented to physicians abroad, we could refer to clinical tests where eight thousand patients in controlled studies in some twenty countries had shown positive results. Plendil has shown itself to be a very effective blood pressure reducing drug with few side effects.

The development of Plendil is an interesting example of how basic research can be used to start a goal-oriented project. The funds that were spent on basic research have paid dividends in the form of a medicine of great value which has also provided the country with export earnings.

Björn Folkow's contributions during the thirty years we have worked together have been of priceless value. For me personally, this work has given me an insight that I only appreciated much later. He got me to realize the importance of living and working closely with basic research. He got me to understand that even goal-oriented research projects require the same competence and creativity needed for basic research. In a newspaper commentary he wrote: "Both within goal-oriented research and in development projects, you have to build on the branches that have grown on the tree of basic research. It is really just the time perspective that separates basic research from goal-oriented research."

Björn believed that there are great risks in narrowly limiting yourself to development projects and short-term goals, as we did at Hässle during the 50's. With such an orientation, there is a risk that the skills of researchers and technicians decline and creativity withers away. It is necessary to keep the stimulation from basic research alive. In another article he wrote:

"It would be like cutting off the branches from a fruit tree and believing that they could bear fruit. They might bloom for a while, if they're put in water, but they can never bear fruit. The fruit tree of knowledge is inseparable. The branches must receive nourishment from the roots."

Perhaps it was my efforts to apply Björn Folkow's philosophy that kept researchers at Hässle, where they developed several successful medicines. Despite the extremely small resources we had during the 50's, 60's, and 70's, these scientists succeeded in developing medicines that are among the most used in the world. Several of these drugs have been licensed to major international companies with more than ten times our research and development budgets.

It is truly not how much money you spend that creates the right atmosphere for creativity and productivity. Competence built-up and maintained in co-operation with university researchers, together with a positive climate for innovation are more important than large resources.

The Effect and Value of Medicines

In the Summer of 1955 we were contacted by the British pharmaceutical company Calmic. A charming Englishman succeeded in convincing me that Calmic's Ferromyn was the world's best iron supplement. He referred to an article in the respected "British Medical Journal". Test results seemed to indicate that Ferromyn caused less side effects, and at the same time had a better effect than the standard supplement with which it was compared.

If we obtained the rights to sell Ferromyn in Sweden, I thought it could be our first effective and well-documented medicine.

On the advice of Björn Folkow, I contacted Leif Hallberg at Gothenburg's Sahlgrenska University Hospital. He was then an assistant professor and later became Professor of Medicine and Supervising Physician.

My first contact with Leif Hallberg was an important turning point on our road to better understanding of the properties of medicines. He taught me to avoid uncritically accepting and believing published studies. I also received an insight into how a drug should be tested and evaluated using scientific methods.

When Leif Hallberg read Calmic's brochure and the article in the British journal, he looked thoughtful. He seemed to be pondering how he should tell the enthusiastic man who believed so strongly in the drug, that it wasn't possible to draw any conclusions from the publicised study. After a while he said:

"It is possible that Ferromyn is better than the standard supplement used for comparison. It may be better than the iron supplements currently sold in Sweden, but this article proves nothing. You can't draw any conclusions from this study."

In my disappointment, I tried to find counter-arguments:

"The British Medical Journal is a serious and respected publication. It wouldn't publish an article with erroneous results. These figures actually show that Ferromyn provides better absorption of iron than other supplements. There are also less side effects."

With great patience, Leif explained:

"The fault in the study is that they have compared a dose of Ferromyn containing 105 milligrams of iron with 200 milligrams of iron in the standard supplement. The reason they give is that these are the recommended doses for both supplements.

"They have measured the increase in the level of the hemoglobin (Hb) in the blood. Then they've calculated how much the Hb increased in proportion to the dose of iron that was given. The doctor who carried out the study hasn't taken up the fact that there is a higher percentage of absorption from a low dose of iron than from a higher dose. That's why it looks like Ferromyn is better. It's also obvious that a lower dose of iron results in less side effects than a high dose. No, you can't draw any conclusions from this publication."

Leif sat quietly for a moment. Then he suggested how we could work together:

"I'm planning to develop a new method to study how iron is absorbed from the intestine into the blood. I want to find the factors that influence this process in order to give the best possible treatment to patients with iron deficency anaemia which is common among women."

"The method I want to work with is based on using very small amounts of (radioactive) isotope-labelled iron. This gives off so little radiation that it is completely harmless, but can still be measured with very sensitive equipment. By marking two preparations with different iron isotopes you could find out, safely, how well one is absorbed compared to the another. If Hässle wants to support that research by contributing the equipment for measuring radiation from iron isotopes, we can work together. Then we can find out if Ferromyn really is an effective supplement."

That conversation was the beginning of a collaboration stretching over many years.

50

It took Leif Hallberg and his colleagues three years of concentrated work to develop a reliable method for measuring iron in blood tests, using the double isotope technique.

When we studied the absorption of iron from Ferromyn using this new method, it turned out that the substance wasn't much better than the standard supplement, contrary to the claim in the British Medical Journal. This research, however, later inspired us to improve Ferromyn. But before we started on that project, we tried to produce a new iron supplement which would be significantly better than all others on the market. We hoped to patent this new supplement, which we expected to be our first international product.

Ferromyn contained an iron salt based on succinic acid. It turned out that if you added significantly higher amounts of succinic acid than was found in the salt, absorption was even better. Adding vitamin C, ascorbic acid, further increased the absorption.

The new supplement, which was called Sorbifer, contained both succinic acid and ascorbic acid to provide the greatest possible iron absorption. The principle was patented.

While the clinical studies were being carried out, we were visited by the President of Astra's American subsidiary, Börje Jalar. He was a vigorous executive who in a short period, and with practically no money from the parent company in Sweden, had built up the American subsidiary into one of the Group's most profitable companies. He was impressed with the research we at Hässle were carrying out in cooperation with the Sahlgrenska Hospital. On a visit to Leif Hallberg's department, Börje Jalar was fascinated by the isotope equipment and the research results he saw. With characteristic dignity, he remarked:

"This iron supplement Sorbifer sounds very interesting. Astra USA is a very successful company because we have marketed the world's best local anaesthetic, Xylocain. The problem for us is that the patent on Xylocain is about to run out. We need a new drug with good patent protection. If Sorbifer lives up to what these results indicate, it could be very valuable to us."

We agreed that Leif Hallberg would visit Astra USA in Worchester, Massachusetts. Together with the company's Vice President, Mats Nilsson, he would meet with various specialists to discuss clinical tests of Sorbifer at a number of American hospitals. Mats and Leif worked well together, and several clinical tests were soon underway.

After a while we received reports of occasional side effects in the American tests. Some patients taking Sorbifer had suffered stomach pains. At about the same time we received similar reports from the Swedish tests. They were so few that at the beginning we were reluctant to believe they were caused by the supplement. Unfortunately, a careful study showed that in certain cases Sorbifer did cause stomach pains. All tests in the United States and Sweden were halted. Our dream of a product for the international market came to nothing. Even worse, Mats Nilsson lost faith in us. He was disappointed that he had been enticed to devote resources and money on a drug that didn't come up to expectations.

The First Million-Seller

The studies carried out by Leif Hallberg and his colleague Lennart Sölvell revealed that it was primarily large doses of ascorbic acid that, together with iron, caused stomach pains. It was suggested that Ferromyn might be improved by adding the right amount of succinic acid, and not using ascorbic acid at all. The goal was to increase iron absorption without causing stomach pains. The new medicine, which was called Ferromyn S, was the biggest selling iron supplement on the Swedish market for several years. It was Hässle's first drug with annual sales of one million kronor (125,000 USD).

The double isotope technique, which was developed at Leif Hallberg's department, made it possible several years later to develop and document the iron supplement Duroferon, which was based on Hässle's own timed-release technique, called Durules. This is probably the best documented iron supplement that exists with regard to reporting on the effect and side effects. This was confirmed for us when experts at the World Health Organization gave the supplement a high rating.

Work with iron supplements during the 50's and 60's taught us how important it is when developing new drugs to have access to accurate methods to test on both healthy persons and patients in order to measure the effect and determine the risk of side effects. It is only with such methods that you can evaluate a drug properly and determine if it is worth introducing onto the market as a new medicine.

Leif Hallberg's clinical experience and creativity was of major importance for our company's development during the 50's and 60's. Not least because of the symposiums he initiated in the early 60's.

He often stressed that the pharmaceutical industry ought to find better ways to maintain contact with physicians than through the traditional advertisements and office visits. At that time our representatives often lacked the proper training to gain the respect of the physicians they visited.

Discussions of these problems led Hässle's Marketing Director Kjell Holmquist to re-evaluate the marketing of our products. He introduced better training for our representatives. Many years collaboration with the Swiss pharmaceutical company Geigy had given him valuable insights into ethical marketing via well-trained representatives. In an interview in December 1983, our board chairman Sten Gustafsson stressed how important it was for Kjell Holmquist to have been able to study modern pharmaceutical marketing through our work with Geigy. It was the way that Kjell applied this experience that made Hässle a market leader in Sweden.

Today, consultants from the pharmaceutical industry are well-trained specialists who present new medicines and clinical results at seminars and hospital round-tables. During the 70's, Hässle was somewhat of a pioneer of ethical marketing in Sweden and providing expert information to physicians.

The Nordic symposiums, which Hässle organized every other year in Gothenburg on Leif Hallberg's initiative, became a means for us to better understand physicians' needs for improved medicines. When the lectures and discussions were published, these books were important in informing physicians in the Nordic countries about current medical problems. They also meant good-will for Hässle.

It was at such a symposium in March 1966 that the idea for our ulcer project was born. This led to the ulcer medicine omeprazol (Losec), which was first marketed internationally in 1988, and which now, in the 90's, is regarded as Astra's most important product.

Constructive Criticism

When I give lectures about product development and management, I usually call attention to an important prerequisite for success: within a project there must always be a balance between innovators, entrepreneurs and constructive critics.

The innovators are researchers and technicians, the creative spirits. They are the ones who create the ideas for new products.

The entrepreneur is the leader who carries the project to its conclusion.

The constructive critic questions the ideas, goals and ways of reaching those goals.

Most of the projects which haven't achieved their goals, and can therefore be regarded as failures, have probably lacked critics. And if critics were involved, then the innovators and entrepreneurs may not have listened to them.

When I go through the minutes and notes from our fumbling efforts at new projects in my first years at Hässle, it is obvious that we lacked a critic who would have forced us to re-evaluate our ideas at an early stage. This is probably the case in most companies where a lot of money is spent on projects over several years without the expected result being achieved.

One interesting example of a project that lacked critics was Astra's fish protein, the Group's most expensive project during the 50's and 60's. Before it was discontinued in the mid-70's, the costs must have easily exceeded 100 million kronor (13 million USD).

A comparison with Hässle's projects that led to the creation of alprenolol and metoprolol might put this figure into perspective.

When alprenolol was registered in Sweden in 1967, the project costs were estimated to have reached 7 million kronor (about one million USD). When metoprolol was registered in 1975, the project costs were estimated at 25 million kronor (3 million USD). Later clinical tests that were carried out for the international marketing of alprenolol and metoprolol probably cost 3 and 5 million USD respectively. So the fish protein project was more expensive than the total costs for the two successful projects that gave the Group alprenolol and metoprolol.

During the years before the registration of alprenolol and metoprolol, we fought hard to get better resources for the project. But that effort was in vain. One reason seems to have been that the fish protein project consumed so much money.

This project was started by a very competent innovator. A university researcher was engaged to solve what were often difficult scientific problems. An energetic entrepreneur succeeded in interesting the Head of the Astra Group in the project.

Sven-Arne Norlindh, who left his position as Hässle's President at the beginning of 1968, was responsible for the fish protein project for several years. In an interview in 1982 he said that Jacob Wallenberg (one of the two heads of Sweden's largest private business empire) had at one point complained that the information he was receiving about the project was too one-sided. He felt that the picture painted was too positive. Sven-Arne Norlindh agreed. He began to play the critic's role and the picture he presented was far different from the entrepreneur's.

As a result, Astra discontinued the project. The entrepreneur and some of the other participants were so convinced about its value, however, that they used their own money to continue on a small scale by selling the protein to organizations who gave protein-enriched flour to countries that had suffered disasters.

There were no critics involved in the project, no one who seriously questioned the goals and potential of marketing the product that was being developed. At the Group's annual research conferences the project was often severely criticised by the heads of research from the pharmaceutical companies. But the entrepreneur didn't listen.

I remember the disinclination to listen to critics during my first years with the company, around 1960, when with naive optimism, we started a number of ill-conceived projects. Lennart Sölvell was the critic who forced us to re-evaluate all of them. As Assistant Professor in Experimental Medicine, he became head of Hässle's Medical Department in 1961.

My first contact with Lennart Sölvell took place as early as 1957 when he was then at Gothenburg's University Hospital. He became a consultant for Hässle and in the beginning worked mostly with the evaluation of substances we could obtain under license from foreign pharmaceutical companies. He also advised us on the planning of clinical tests. At an early stage, he teamed up with John Sjögren, a young pharmacist employed at Hässle. Together they created several medically important products. It was these preparations that gave the company the economic ability to develop resources for more advanced research.

As the responsible medical chief, Lennart Sölvell became more and more critical of the research projects we were pursuing. I have to admit that in the beginning it was far from pleasant when he questioned every one of our research projects. But after a few months, I realized that his criticism was justified. We agreed that it was necessary to review not only our objectives, but also the methods used for the evaluation of the substances we were synthesizing. In a short time, he had carried out tests on healthy people with the substances we had hoped would be valuable medicines, but not a single one turned out to be worth developing.

In the Fall of 1961, we reached an important turning point. We realized that we didn't know enough to take new chemical compounds from the animal studies stage to tests, first on healthy people, and then on patients. We had to work out how to set up the research from the beginning so that all the safety aspects were observed. How should we structure the research projects that would give us new medicines where the clinical advantages clearly outweighed the risks of side effects?

There was nothing in the literature that could help us. When I asked the head of research at our facility in Södertälje for help he told me that their main experience was in evaluating and clinically testing lidocain (Xylocain) and other local anaesthetics. That experience was of no use to us in projects developing drugs for the treatment of heart disease and diseases of the central nervous system. These were the fields in which we started to work in the early 60's.

Lennart and I received permission from the board of directors to visit foreign pharmaceutical companies to try to learn from their experience.

In the Spring of 1962 we visited a number of companies in Belgium, Britain, Switzerland and West Germany. The following Fall, during a six week trip in the United States, we met researchers at nine more companies.

It was a varied picture we encountered as we visited different companies. At most the researchers were very open. They thought it was interesting to talk with the clinical scientist Sölvell, who was obviously ready to reconsider the methods we had been using. The authorities in many countries hadn't yet drawn up new safety regulations after the thalidomide tragedy and there was great uncertainty about how such problems could be solved.

The toxicologists and other researchers we visited shared with us their companies' policies and the safety regulations they followed. The most rewarding visits were to the British company ICI and Upjohn in the United States. Both companies had already introduced control systems that would easily satisfy the stringent standards that the authorities in those countries later introduced.

In his report, Lennart Sölvell summarized our study visits in Europe and the United States. This became the basis for the policies and safety standards we developed for testing new chemical substances on healthy people and for setting up clinical studies to determine if new substances could become useful medicines.

But in May 1962, Lennart Sölvell told me that he had applied for the position of Assistant Chief Physician at the University Hospital. He expected to leave Hässle that Fall. He said he had tested all the interesting compounds our chemists had produced. None of them had shown enough positive effects to motivate going on. None of our projects had any promising compounds left, so there was really nothing left for a clinical scientist to do.

This came as a considerable shock to me. I had come to value Lennart's role as a discerning critic. He had gotten me to re-evaluate practically everything we were doing within research and product development.

If Lennart left, my only conclusion had to be that he no longer believed in Hässle's ability to create useful medicines. When he saw the great resources of the international pharmaceutical companies during our study visits, he must have decided it would be impossible for Hässle to compete with them since they had ten to twenty times our resources.

But there was another reason why Lennart Sölvell wanted to leave Hässle. He sounded disappointed when he told me:

"I have a strong feeling that the pharmaceutical industry in this country isn't really interested in employing a clinical scientist. Maybe they think we are too critical. As an Assistant Chief Physician, I'll get a much higher salary than I get here. Ordinarily academics are paid higher salaries in industry than in the public sector but not here.

"If the company is prepared to pay me the same salary as an Assistant Chief Physician, I would see that as a sign they really want a clinical scientist. I would see it as support for my critical approach to some aspects of our activities and for my efforts towards finding new ways to create better medicines."

I felt relieved, and saw a chance to keep him:

"That shouldn't be a problem. It's obvious that we need a clinical scientist for our research and we would have to pay at least whatever a hospital pays. But Hässle's management can't make that decision by itself. We have to have the approval of the Group management."

Hässle's President, Sven-Arne Norlindh, was unequivocally positive. He telephoned the Group's vice president while I was on an extension, but to our dismay the response was disappointing:

"None of our doctors in Södertälje has that high a salary. We can't accept Hässle paying higher salaries than we pay here. Sölvell will have to wait for his raise."

Sven-Arne and I had strong counter arguments:

"For the first time the Astra Group, and perhaps the entire Swedish pharmaceutical industry, has managed to hire a clinical scientist with these kind of academic credentials. We have to do everything we can to keep him. We can't help it if you don't have another doctor of his calibre anywhere else in the Group. That shouldn't be a deciding factor. Sölvell is far too important for our research."

But no argument worked, the answer was still no. Lennart turned in his resignation.

That evening I took a long walk in the forest. It was one of the few times during my twenty-four years as Research Director that I was on the verge of giving up. I was sure it would be impossible for us to carry out our projects without the help of a competent clinical scientist. We are trying to find medicines that would help patients. How could we do that without the help of a doctor with good clinical experience? How could I handle the discussions with enthusiastic researchers and innovators without the assistance of a competent clinical scientist? The next day I outlined a plan to Lennart.

"I think it's impossible to continue our research without your help. I'm appalled at the reaction of Group management. They obviously don't understand how important it is to have a clinical scientist involved in our projects all the way from conception to the creation of a final medicine.

"Of course we could hire consultants, clinical scientists at the hospital. But there's such a huge difference between giving advice from outside and being part of the work and taking responsibility. We need you onboard if we're going to cope with these projects. I have a proposal for how we can make the best out of a difficult situation, if you have to leave us in the Fall."

Lennart looked relieved. "Let's hear it."

"First of all, I hope you'll go on your planned study visit to the United States in the Fall. Then I want to work out an agreement where you can continue to help me as an advisor. We can formally agree that you'll work for us a certain number of hours a week. We'll pay you a consultant fee for your time. When and where you do your work for us doesn't matter. We can meet at your house, at the hospital, or here at Hässle with the researchers."

Lennart agreed completely with the proposal.

"I obviously want to go on the study visit we've planned to the American pharmaceutical companies. The visits to companies in Britain, Belgium and Switzerland were very rewarding. We ought to be able to find a way for me to continue to help you evaluate projects and the substances the chemists produce."

During my remaining fifteen years as Research Director, Lennart Sölvell was my advisor and critic. He also helped me compile our annual research reports. Without his participation at the Group's research conferences, it's doubtful if I would have succeeded in getting projects approved by that critical forum, which was composed of the research directors of the Group's Research and Development organizations and the five professors the board had commissioned to monitor our activities.

A New Road Toward the Goal

When I realized in the spring of 1961 that we had to reappraise our goals and our methods of reaching them in our research projects, I sought contact with Arvid Carlsson. As Assistant Professor in the Pharmacological Department at the University of Lund he had explored other forms of research than pharmacologists traditionally work with.

During a year as guest researcher at the National Institute of Health in Washington, he had become interested in the biochemical mechanisms of the central nervous system. He became one of the leading researchers within this new field which aims to clarify how the brain's nerve cells communicate with each other using signal substances as messengers.

Arvid Carlsson's discovery of the role of the signal substance dopamine in treating the difficult mental disorders we call psychoses and it's role for Parkinson's Disease led to the development of the medicine L-dopa used to alleviate the latter sickness. The psychopharmacological research that was carried out first by Hässle and then by Astra was based on the work done at Arvid Carlsson's department.

In the Fall of 1959, Arvid Carlsson became Professor and Head of the Department of Pharmacology at the University of Gothenburg. Once in 1960, I consulted Arvid to find a solution to a problem that had stalled one of our research projects. In May 1961 I asked him to undertake a one day review of our entire research program.

After Lennart Sölvell's critical review of our research projects, we were ready to discuss the entire program with Arvid Carlsson. During that day I presented the six projects we were working with and at the end, Arvid summarized his impressions:

"It's been interesting to see how you work at Hässle. It's clear you have very creative chemists."

But I realized that Arvid was not telling the whole truth. He probably didn't want to criticize me, after I had, perhaps too enthusiastically, described the projects we had been working on for two years. After a few moments' thought while I gathered up my papers with our tables and diagrams, I asked:

"If you, Arvid, were in my shoes, and were responsible for Hässle's research, what would you do now?"

Arvid looked thoughtful and finally answered:

"I would probably throw out the projects you're working on. If you use the same biological test methods that the researchers at other companies use, you can hardly expect to develop completely new drugs with different mechanisms. Skilled chemists can develop variations on drugs that already exist. Of course those can have some advantages, but you rarely find anything really new that way. You should work from new biological mechanisms.

"As far as choosing projects goes, I would never look for a particular indication, like heart rhythms. Instead of restricting the project's goals to the symptom heart rhythms, I would study the mechanisms that control the activities of the heart. By studying the factors that influence the heart rhythm and the work of the heart muscle, you can hope to develop medicines for different heart diseases."

This way of organizing research means that, from the very beginning, you give the project a more biological orientation than is usual within the pharmaceuticals industry. Until then, drug research had primarily been run by chemists. This new direction suggested by Arvid fascinated me:

"If we work in the way you suggest, could you consider being our consultant, and help us find the right direction?"

That was the beginning of a long and fruitful co-operation. Although after Astra moved the psychopharmaca project to Södertälje, contacts between Hässle and Arvid Carlsson became less frequent.

Arvid Carlsson's outline of our research in May 1961 was one of the most important turning points in our progress towards developing better medicines. The projects that were based on this philosophy had great importance, not just for Hässle's research, but also for the entire Astra Group.

As a result, Hässle created several extremely important medicines for the treatment of heart diseases and high blood pressure.

On Arvid Carlsson's advice we also began to study the adrenergic mechanism's effect on bronchi in the Fall of 1961, in the hope of developing a better drug for the treatment of asthma. By 1966 we'd produced a promising substance which we planned to use for human tests. But the Group's research conference in September 1966 recommended that the asthma project be discontinued so that Hässle could concentrate its resources on medicines to fight heart disease. As a result this substance was never tested on humans.

Our sister company, Draco, eventually started research in to drugs for the treatment of asthma along the lines suggested by Arvid Carlsson. Draco's pharmacologist, Henry Persson worked at Hässle's pharmacology lab in 1962-63, where he took part in a project involving adrenergic mechanisms, mechanisms that govern the effect of the hormone adrenaline on the heart and other organs. Henry was responsible for Draco's biological work, and together with the company's chemists he created the asthma medicine Bricanyl, based on his own ideas on how the effects on the heart and lungs could be separated.

Arvid Carlsson's recommendations were a turning point, and his ideas about how psychopharmacological research should be carried out also had a great importance for Astra's research in Södertälje.

Before Astra came in contact with Arvid Carlsson at our project meetings in the 60's, the psychopharmacological research at Södertälje was mainly carried out along the same lines as projects initiated by chemists at other pharmaceutical companies. You started from new chemical structures and tried to use them to find clues that would lead to new medicines for different sicknesses. The research in the field carried out after Astra came in contact with Arvid Carlsson rests on the biological path he gave us.

As late as the 70's, several international pharmaceutical companies continued to let chemists dominate their drug research.

At a symposium in Italy in 1982 Arvid Carlsson and I had an opportunity to present our work and its results together. It was interesting to see how the other symposium participants regarded our way of starting with biological mechanisms as something new. Our talks and the following discussions were published in the book "Decision Making in Drug Research". The pharmacologist Franz Gross commented on the book in the "British Medical Journal" under the headline: "Drug Research: Dead End or New Horizon?". Gross meant that as drug research became more and more expensive to carry out, it must find new directions. He wrote:

"A stimulating concept, presented at the symposium, was the attempt to create new drugs by starting with biological hypotheses, and using chemical compounds to clarify biological mechanisms... This can lead to new types of medicines."

Franz Gross referred to the work being done in Gothenburg: "where a company is successfully working together with university scientists."

This was written more than twenty years after Arvid Carlsson gave us the advice to start with biological mechanisms and test our substances with new pharmacological methods. This principle of looking for worthwhile medicines was also to guide us in 1966 when we started a project to find medicines to treat stomach ulcers.

When the British pharmacologist, James Black, won the Nobel Prize in 1988 for creating the heart medicine Inderal and the ulcer medicine Tagamet, he shared the prize with two other scientists who had worked within totally different areas of drug research. The official motivation for awarding the prize to these researchers was:

"What is characteristic of all three laureates is that in their research they have started from increased knowledge of the body's natural processes and then looked for ways of influencing these functions. This makes for more effective research and more direct-acting medicines."

This is just another way of describing the way we worked after May 1961.

Disasters and Tragedies

"The Harmless Sleeping Pill"

Few things have had such an effect on the research programs in the pharmaceutical industry as the Thalidomide disaster. Besides forcing us to develop better safety tests for drugs before they could be allowed to be used on patients, we also realized we had to know more about how our drugs worked.

When the cause of the catastrophe was discovered in 1961, it changed the work of the drug researcher completely.

Thalidomide was developed in the mid-50's. Researchers at the German pharmaceutical company Chemie-Grönenthal were convinced that their new drug was completely safe. Despite large amounts given to mice and rats, they couldn't find a fatal dose. Nor had they seen any injurious effects on other animals. Finally, a safe sedative!

For decades barbiturates had been more or less the only drugs available to induce sleep. The first was phenobarbital, followed by pentobarbital. But even small doses of these were all a would-be suicide needed to succeed. Only if the unconscious person was found in time, with the empty pill bottle on the night stand, could a stomach pump save his or her life.

There was a dramatic example of the new drug's harmlessness during the clinical tests in West Germany in 1954 and 1955. A young man trying to commit suicide swallowed more than a hundred tablets. It was certainly difficult to wake him up afterwards, but when he had, the doctors couldn't find any signs of injuries.

But, Thalidomide wasn't just going to be the harmless sleeping-drug. It also seemed to have a tranquilizing effect when given to patients with nervous conditions. No disturbing side effects had been reported.

Naturally the researchers were enthusiastic, and the company management saw an opportunity for major sales. There was a considerable need for a sleeping-drug and tranquilizer in post-war Germany and other countries.

When Thalidomide was first sold in West Germany in October 1957, under the name Contergan, it was presented as "the sleeping-drug of the century". It was said to be "a safe and non-toxic tranquilizer and sleeping-drug". It was sold without prescription at German pharmacies.

The drug was a great success in West Germany. In 1961, four years after its introduction, it was estimated that a million Germans used Contergan.

One of Hässle's scientific consultants had heard about the positive results of the clinical tests of Thalidomide during a trip to West Germany in early 1958. In a letter to me he recommended that we try to get the licensing rights for this "harmless sleeping-drug". When Chemie-Grünenthal answered my letter inquiring about the rights to tell me that another Swedish company had already received the licensing for Sweden, Denmark, and Norway, I was disappointed. Later I discovered that it was our parent company Astra which had received the license to sell Thalidomide in Scandinavia!

In the minutes of the Astra Board of Directors meeting on October 15, 1957, it was noted that an agreement had been signed with Chemie-Grönenthal giving Astra the right to sell Thalidomide in Scandinavia and several other countries. One and half years later, on April 25, 1959, Group president reported to Astra's Board that the sleeping-drug Thalidomide was being marketed in Sweden, under the name of Neurosedyn. The president was pleased to tell the Board that physicians had shown great interest in this "harmless" sleeping-drug. However, unlike most other countries, a prescription was required for Thalidomide in Sweden.

No one could have imagined that the name Thalidomide would forever be remembered as one of medicine's greatest disasters.

Within a short period Chemie-Grünenthal signed licensing agreements covering most of the world. Thalidomide was sold under various names in more than fifty countries.

The drug was never marketed in the United States. The American pharmaceutical company Smith, Kline & French (SK&F) signed a licensing agreement at an early date. But after clinical tests in 1957, SK&F said that "Thalidomide had no advantages" over other tranquilizing drugs. So the agreement with the German company was cancelled.

Astra was then offered the licensing rights for the American market. Fortunately, Astra's American subsidiary refused to even begin clinical tests. Börje Jalar was the President of Astra's American subsidiary between 1949 and 1963. Looking back in the Summer of 1988, he said:

"Both the company management back in Sweden and experts from Chemie-Grünenthal tried to convince me that we should market Thalidomide the American market. But I refused. I relied completely upon our Research Director Aldo Truant. He rejected the animal experiments the Germans had carried out. He didn't think any certain conclusions could be drawn from them. You can imagine what it would have meant for our company in the United States if Astra had been part of the tragedy that followed when the damage caused by Thalidomide was discovered."

Astra can truly thank Aldo Truant, but it ought to be stressed that even he hadn't foreseen the risk of foetal defects and other side effects that were later discovered. He was merely sceptical of the results presented in the German reports. He thought that the scientific quality was unacceptable. Considering our experiences at Hässle with other German companies during the 60's, it's easy to understand his reaction. In the German pharmaceutical industry, chemists completely dominated both research and management, so pharmacologists and physicians had great difficulty in making themselves heard.

It was Rickardson Merrell Inc. which finally took on the licensing for Thalidomide in the United States. The company started the most comprehensive program for clinical tests that had ever been carried out on a new drug. More than one thousand doctors gave the trial drug to nearly 30,000 patients. It was a totally irresponsible way to test a drug that the authorities had yet to approve.

Thanks to Dr. Frances Kelsey's suspicions concerning the German animal tests, Thalidomide was never approved for marketing in the United States. Dr. Kelsey was the Food and Drug Administration official responsible for the evaluation of the documentation for Thalidomide. It seems to have been her first assignment for the FDA. Her husband, who was also a doctor and pharmacologist, also thought the German reports were deficient. The FDA stopped the use of Thalidomide in the United States for the same reason that Astra's Research Director Aldo Truant had recommended that we refrain from clinical tests.

Dr. Kelsey's suspicions certainly prevented a major medical catastrophe in the United States. She received a medal from President Kennedy for her efforts.

Merrel was involved in many court cases involving demands for large-scale damages because of the foetal defects that resulted from doctors' prescribing Thalidomide to pregnant women during the clinical tests.

It was here that Sweden became inextricably linked with Thalidomide in the American consciousness when housewife Sherry Finkbine, one of the women who had taken Thalidomide while pregnant, had to travel to Sweden for an abortion, which was then illegal in the United States.

A Mysterious Epidemic and Its Cause

Between 1959 and 1961 there was a disturbing increase in the number of West German children born with birth defects. Before 1959 children had been born with deformed arms, hands, and legs. But in two years the number had risen so quickly that it began to be described as an epidemic.

As more and more reports came of children born without arms, and sometimes without legs as well, there was an intense debate in the German press about the cause. Radioactive radiation from nuclear weapons tests or reactors, or toxins in the environment, food, or water, were all cited as possible reasons. The mass media interviewed countless scientists and politicians in an effort to be the first to reveal the cause. In many cases the birth defects were similar to those that had occurred before, but some resulted in far more serious handicaps.

The story of how it was finally discovered that Thalidomide was the "culprit" reads like a detective thriller. It's also an example of how difficult it is for people to believe the unexpected. When it doesn't fit established views. According to the conventional knowledge of the time, a drug could not be transmitted from a mother's blood to a foetus. The protective barriers were supposed to be so effective that there was no need to fear damage. So no one looked for a drug taken by pregnant women as the cause of the increase in birth defects. When the first reports came, indicating a link between Thalidomide and birth defects, scientists simply refused to accept it.

It was not a doctor, but rather a lawyer who first uncovered the truth.

In March 1961 the young German lawyer Karl Schulte-Hillen saw his sister's newborn child. It was a shocking experience. The girl had no arms. Her hands, missing both thumbs and index fingers, were attached directly to her shoulders. In order to avoid worrying his own wife, who was also pregnant, he said nothing to her about his sister's deformed child. Six weeks later Schulte-Hillen's wife gave birth to a son with the same deformed arms and hands.

Since both his own and his sister's children had the same deformity, at first Schulte-Hillen thought some strange hereditary characteristic was responsible. When he couldn't find similar deformities in his family history, he began to look for other causes. The doctor who delivered his wife said: "All parents of deformed children look for external factors. But it's useless to look for causes." The energetic lawyer didn't give up, however. He realized he needed the help of a physician. A friend recommended that he contact paediatrician Widukind Lenz, head of Hamburg's University Hospital's children's clinic.

Dr. Lenz was sceptical of the lawyer's theory that some medicine might be the cause of both children's deformities. When Hillen asked his sister if she had taken any medicine during her pregnancy, she remembered that on two nights she had taken a sedative she had gotten from a friend. That was Contergan, which was available without prescription from pharmacies.

The lawyer had already found out that his wife had received a tranquilizer from her sister the night the two of them had sat together beside their father's deathbed. His wife had never before or after taken a tranquilizer or sleeping pill. That drug was also Contergan.

When Hillen told him this, Dr. Lenz agreed to help him try to establish if Contergan was dangerous to give to pregnant women. As time went by, the lawyer found more cases of deformed children where the

69

mother had taken Contergan in the early stages of pregnancy.

Dr. Lenz became very interested. He contacted different hospitals. By November 1961 he had reports of 16 cases of birth defects in which the mother had taken Contergan.

On November 15th the doctor called the Research Director at Chemie-Grünenthal, Dr. Heinrich Mückter. He asked that Contegan be immediately removed from the market because of the probability that it had caused serious foetal defects. Dr. Mückter was sceptical that the "harmless" drug Contergan could be responsible. He had no intention of recommending that his company withdraw the drug.

On November 19th Dr. Lenz took part in a pediatrians' conference in Dusseldorf. In a lecture he reported on the strong suspicion that 16 deformed children had been born after their mothers had taken a certain drug. He didn't say which drug, because he didn't think he had enough evidence. He ended the lecture with the warning: "Every month we don't do anything means 50 to 100 deformed children will be born in West Germany."

After the lecture Dr. Lenz was contacted by a colleague who asked: "Do you mean Contergan? My wife took Contergan, and she gave birth to a deformed child."

On Monday November 20th Dr. Lenz presented to the healthcare authorities in Hamburg his suspicions that Contergan caused birth defects. Schulte-Hillen came to the meeting with the physician. Chemie-Grünenthal's representatives tried to force the lawyer to leave the meeting because he wasn't a doctor. The company representatives refused to accept the suggestion that Contergan be withdrawn from the market, but did accept putting the warning text "Should not be taken by pregnant women" on the bottles.

The same day as the meeting, Research Director Mückter received a letter from the company holding the British license to sell Thalidomide, Distillers. It described how a Dr. McBride in Australia had reported 6 cases of birth defects in which the mothers had all taken Thalidomide.

On Sunday November 26th the newspaper "Welt am Sonntag" reported on Dr. Lenz' findings which the newspaper had obtained without the physician's knowledge.

The article hit Chemie-Grünenthal like a bombshell. There was panic. With the 16 cases Dr. Lenz had uncovered and the 6 cases from Australia, it was obvious that something had to be done. The company knew, of course, of the fear in West Germany because of the large number of children born with birth defects during the past two years. That "Welt am Sonntag" now thought it could name the cause was a sensation.

That same day, company management sent a telegram to the German Interior Ministry: "Until the questions that have arisen have been scientifically examined, we have decided to withdraw Contergan from the market, effective immediately". Eleven days had elapsed between Dr. Lenz' call to Research Director Möckter and the decision to withdraw Contergan from sales in West Germany on November 26th.

Those eleven days were tragically critical to one West German woman who had trouble sleeping and bought Contergan at a pharmacy while it was still on the shelves. On each of the nights of November 20th and 21st she took a tablet. Eight months later, on July 22, 1962, she gave birth to a severely deformed child who died after two days. Since the tablets had been taken during the first month of pregnancy, when she hadn't even known she was pregnant, a warning for pregnant women not to take the drug would have been meaningless.

After the drug was withdrawn from the market in West Germany on November 26, 1961, several other countries followed suit. In Japan, however, this would not be until the Summer of 1962. One reason for the delay was probably because Chemie-Grönenthal wrote in a letter to the Japanese license-holder that there was no evidence of a connection between Contergan and birth defects. The company claimed that a warning that pregnant women should not take the drug would be sufficient.

It is estimated that in West Germany alone, 5,000 deformed children were born after their mothers took Contergan. The world-wide total has been estimated at nearly 10,000. It was a terrible medical catastrophe.

No Suspicions in Sweden

In Sweden there was no worry about an epidemic causing birth defects. The atmosphere of fear that prevailed in West Germany did not spread to Sweden. During the years 1959 to 1961, when Thalidomide was on the Swedish market, more than 100,000 children were born annually. Afterwards it was calculated that during that period the number of children born with birth defects increased from 12 to 18 per 1,000 births. No one noticed anything unusual. To a certain extent this was probably because, at that time, the system of reporting on side effects and birth defects was less effective than it is today.

The day after "Welt am Sonntag" published the sensational article saying that Contergan caused birth defects, a few Swedish newspapers printed short articles. It was obvious that none of the journalists thought the German medical disaster affected Swedish readers. One reporter tried to follow up the story and called a local pharmacy to ask if the German drug Contergan was sold in Sweden, but no one knew that Thalidomide was sold in Sweden under another name, Neurosedyn.

Four months later a group of physicians published a report revealing 7 Thalidomide deformities in one city and 5 more in another.

One of the articles on November 27th carried the headline: "Sleeping Tablet Dangerous for Pregnant Women", but neither doctors nor patients seem to have been upset by this warning signal.

On Monday November 27th Astra's Managing Director Arne Wegerfelt read one of the short articles about the birth defects apparently caused by the German sleeping-drug Contergan. Physicians and other specialists in the company assured him that it must be a mistake. A drug couldn't hurt a foetus. The protective barrier between the mother and the foetus was too effective. Dr. Carl-Olof Svedin, Astra's Medical Director, read the news in another paper. He just could not believe that there was anything behind the German newspaper's claim that a drug caused birth defects. However, he asked one of the physicians in the Medical Department to call the German company, but chaos rained at Chemie-Grönenthal. Astra couldn't get a straight answer and asked for a written report.

Dr. Svedin contacted Professor Åke Liljestrand, who was responsible for matters related to drugs at the Swedish Medical Board. He too found it hard to believe that this substance could be harmful. He thought people in West Germany might have used it improperly. It was sold without prescription there which meant that some patients may have taken too large doses. In Sweden, where Thalidomide was only available a doctor's prescription, there was better control over its use. Liljestrand didn't think the drug had to be withdrawn from the Swedish market. Svedin and Liljestrand agreed to send a letter to all doctors with the warning: "Don't give Neurosedyn to pregnant women."

It is worth pointing out that the Medical Board's State Pharmaceutical Laboratory had studied reports of side effects from newly marketed drugs. There were no comments about Neurosedyn which must have been one reason that Åke Liljestrand was sceptical of the German report of side effects. It was just a story in a weekly paper.

In a later commentary, Åke Liljestrand said: "Following the stories in the newspapers, we immediately asked for reports from Chemie-Grönenthal. However, these were not forthcoming until the second week in December."

Both Torsten Romanus, scientific advisor to the Medical Board, and Åke Liljestrand each went through the reports and agreed that there was indeed a new syndrome, probably caused by Contergan.

What no one knew, when this was discussed, was that more than 90 deformed children had already been born in Sweden, where Neurosedyn would later be believed to be responsible.

By December 7, 1961, West Germany, Britain, the Netherlands, and Denmark had all withdrawn Thalidomide products from the market. But in Sweden, both Astra and the State Medical Board hesitated. They found it hard to believe that there really was a connection between the drug and birth defects.

On December 12th, Åke Liljestrand discussed the problem with the Director of the Medical Board, Arthur Engel. Engel thought that Neurosedyn should be withdrawn straight away. Liljestrand agreed and advised Astra to request an immediate deregistration which was the quickest way to remove the drug from the market. The formal decision to withdraw Neurosedyn was made on December 14th. Astra sent a letter to all of the country's doctors and pharmacies. All supplies were returned.

But the public was not warned. Only through a major article in the evening tabloid "Expressen", the country's largest newspaper, was the public alerted to the risk of birth defects. After the drug was withdrawn from the market, five more children were born with birth defects, presumably caused by use of Neurosedyn.

It might appear strange that the press and broadcast media didn't take the withdrawal of a drug that had presumably caused birth defects more seriously. The explanation is probably that there were no reports in Sweden that there was an increase in the number of children born with birth defects as was the case in West Germany. No one in the press had written about birth defects. For the general public, it was a virtually unknown problem. After several weeks of near total silence, the first Neurosedyn story appeared in the press on February 23, 1962. That was a report about five deformed children where it was believed that Neursedyn had caused birth defects.

When a paediatrician later investigated, it turned out that there were more than one hundred deformed children in Sweden where a connection with Neurosedyn was suspected. That caused a lively public debate. But not until then.

Intense Involvement

Altogether, 153 children were born in Sweden with birth defects that are believed to have been caused by Neurosedyn. Around 100 of these children survived, seventy of them with severe handicaps.

When people saw pictures of Swedish children without arms and legs in the newspapers and on television, they were deeply disturbed. Never has a group of handicapped people met so much sympathy as the Neurosedyn children.

Three facilities were set up to take care of the most severe cases.

In the wave of sympathy for the Neurosedyn children and their relatives that followed, people almost forgot that there were already several thousand Swedish children with serious handicaps. Every year many deformed children are born in Sweden. Now demands were made that all these children be treated just as generously as the Neurosedyn children. So the disaster led to greater attention being focused on the problems of handicapped children.

Going through the archives from that time, you gain a picture of how civil servants in the health sector and other agencies, through bureaucratic red tape and plain pettiness, refused to give much-needed financial support to the parents of the Neursedyn children. Long drawn-out disputes went on between bureaucrats about which county authority should pay for the treatment at the three special institutions that had been set up. This delayed, and in some cases prevented, children from receiving the care they needed.

Jan Winberg's Investigation

On December 13, 1961 paediatrician and Assistant Professor Jan Winberg and a group of young physicians left on a study trip to Bonn in West Germany. It was almost three weeks after Contergan had been withdrawn from the German market.

The day before, December 12th, the Director of the State Medical Board, Arthur Engel, had called for Neurosedyn to be withdrawn in Sweden, but Jan Winberg didn't know that. He also didn't know that Astra would call back all supplies of Neurosedyn from pharmacies in Sweden.

In Bonn, Jan Winberg and his young colleagues listened to a German professor lecture on birth defects. He showed two children with deformities for the Swedish group.

Jan Winberg later wrote: "When I saw the children with deformed arms, hands, and feet, I realized that I had seen a similar child in Gothenburg the previous Fall and another the day before I left for Germany. I had wondered what had caused the deformities, but I never suspected a drug."

The German lecturer said that the defects had been caused by the mothers' taking Thalidomide. On his arrival home, Winberg discovered that both of the mothers in Gothenburg had taken Thalidomide in the form of Neurosedyn. He found several more cases in Gothenburg which were probably caused by the drug.

It was now obvious that Sweden had also been affected by the Thalidomide disaster. Jan Winberg was asked by the State Medical Board to study the Neurosedyn defects. Following Astra's introduction of Neurosedyn to the market on February 5, 1959, the first child with the typical Thalidomide defects was born that October, eight months after sales began. In November and December two more deformed children were born, and there was also cause to suspect Neurosedyn. But then, in 1959, there was no suspicion that anything unusual was happening.

Winberg's study revealed that during 1961, forty of the 125,000 children born that year had defects that were typical for Thalidomide. No doctor had suspected that these forty cases of birth defects were caused by a drug.

Jan Winberg summarized in an article in the Swedish Medical Journal in 1969, his findings which: "… were the basis for the newly agreed settlement in the four year-long court case between the parents of the Neurosedyn-deformed children and the pharmaceutical company Astra."

He wrote that he had studied the cases of 123 children who were born with birth defects between the years 1957 and 1964. He had himself examined around twenty of these.

In Sweden, around 2,000 children are born every year with some degree of birth defect. In most cases it is impossible to find a cause. Even where children who were believed to have been deformed by Neursedyn were concerned, it was generally not possible in individual cases to prove that the defect had been caused by the drug.

For one thing, it was often impossible to know if the woman had taken Neurosedyn during the short period in which the foetus could have been damaged by the drug. In many cases the woman had been given a tranquilizer by a friend and she didn't remember what the drug was.

Another reason for the difficulty in proving the connection was that such deformities have always existed without the mothers' taking any drugs. This was a problem above all where less serious deformities were concerned.

The most severely deformed children lacked arms and legs. Hands and feet were attached directly to their shoulders and hips. They were like seals, which led to the name "fokomels", from the Latin "fokemelos" or "seal-limb".

Of the 123 deformed children, Winberg believed that there was a strong suspicion that Neurosedyn was responsible in 88 cases. In 22 cases, there was a probability of another cause. Eleven of the mothers denied taking Neurosedyn. Some of these children had lesser defects, such as deformed ears.

The Neurosedyn Trial

Two parent associations had been organized. They represented the Neurosedyn children in the suits filed against Astra for damages.

The court proceedings in Sweden began in the Fall of 1965. From the beginning, the main problem for the jurists was to prove or even assume a connection between Neurosedyn and the birth defects. Jan Wiberg's study had shown that, in most of the cases, it was impossible to determine if the mothers of the deformed children had taken Neurosedyn during the critical period. An additional problem was that similar deformities had existed before Neurosedyn was marketed. Some of them had deformities similar to those attributed to Neurosedyn.

Lawyers on both sides demanded absolute proof, but it didn't exist. There was an impasse.

Astra's president said to me in 1981:

"I was shocked the first time I saw pictures of children deformed by Neurosedyn. It hurt me deeply that one of our drugs could cause such serious deformities. The fact that a drug that our scientists and experts considered safe could cause severe deformities in foetuses changed my attitude towards drugs."

In various ways we within Astra felt the president's fears that something similar could happen in the future. Naturally he gave his full support for investing resources in developing better methods for improving safety standards and for testing the possible risks of a new drug before it was allowed to be tested on humans. We also saw how he wanted to move away from the company's strong dependence on drugs. It's from this perspective that one should see Arne Wegerfeldt's interest in Astra's fish protein project that would produce a product without dangerous side effects. A non-perishable fish protein, easy to distribute, could save children in poor countries from protein deficiency.

Astra's president did not want the Neurosedyn trials to turn into a campaign to protect the company's reputation. Within Astra there was a dispute over who should be responsible for the legal proceedings. Arne Wegerfelt took the unusual decision of letting Sven Sundling and his associate Bo Teglund handle this difficult assignment, with the help, of course, of medical experts and legal advisors.

Sven Sundling, who came to Astra in 1954, was during the 60's and 70's the company's Information Director. He was Secretary of the Board of Directors, and became Arne Wegerfedlt's close associate and advisor. In the Spring of 1990 he described his role in the Neurosedyn trials:

"There were endless discussions between the families' lawyers and their experts. In the mean time, parents of the deformed children were forced to wait for the economic support they needed.

"At this point, Astra's board chairman Jacob Wallenberg (head of Sweden's most powerful family business empire) intervened personally. He called Arne Wegerfelt and me to a meeting at the Enskilda Bank. With characteristic seriousness, Jacob Wallenberg said: 'You have to arrange a settlement immediately. These proceedings can go on for years. Only the lawyers can profit from that. See that the deformed children's families are paid damages as soon as possible.'"

Sven Sundling continued:

"I constantly worried about how we could reach a settlement. Lawyers on both sides were locked in their positions. In which cases could we be certain that the mothers had taken Neurosedyn? Which could be completely discounted? The discussions circled endlessly around those questions. I had an idea: Astra would offer a total settlement package, but at the same time demand that all the deformed children, where there was the slightest suspicion of a connection with Neurosedyn, would receive compensation. Altogether, 110 children were parties to the claims. We wouldn't bother about proving a connection between their deformities and whether their mothers had taken Neurosedyn. That was Astra's condition for reaching a settlement.

"At first it was difficult to convince our own lawyer that this unusual procedure was the right way. However, Wegerfelt made it clear that this was what Astra was going to do. It was much more difficult to get the other lawyers to accept the settlement. They wanted to go to court. The settlement was finally accepted in 1969. Just the suspicion that a child had been deformed by Neurosedyn was grounds for compensation."

Altogether, Astra paid more than 20 million dollars into the Neurosedyn Fund.

No amount of money, no matter how large, can compensate for the pain and suffering of a such a handicap, but the money from the Neurosedyn Fund must have given important support to the families of the deformed children.

Thanks to then-Finance Minister, Gunnar Sträng's initiative, the Swedish Parliament decided that payments from the Neurosedyn Fund should be tax-free. The deformed children will receive inflation-adjusted compensation payments as long as they live.

Trials in Other Countries

In Britain, the Distillers company was sued for damages and the company's lawyers were completely responsible for the legal proceedings. The strictly formalistic way in which they acted provoked a strong reaction from the public. Several shareholders objected. Among these was an insurance company which demanded a change. The company was forced to settle.

The settlement, which was arrived at earlier than in Sweden, meant that the families of the deformed children received 40 percent of the damages they would have received if they had won in court.

In West Germany the legal proceedings were long and drawn-out. Chemie-Grünenthal's management and Research Director were indicted for negligence and for causing the deformities.

Could the Disaster Have Been Prevented?

Scientists in several countries devoted a great deal of energy finding an animal model which would produce birth defects similar to those seen in the Thalidomide children.

It was only when an British scientist gave Thalidomide to a New Zealand White Rabbit, that the birth defects were duplicated. Much higher doses given to other kinds of rabbits and mice had no effect.

Tests carried out after the Thalidomide disaster show how difficult or nearly impossible it would have been to have demonstrated the risks of birth defects before Thalidomide was marketed. What made it even more improbable to foresee the risks was the belief at the time that such drugs couldn't cause birth defects.

Later tests have shown that several common medicines can cause birth defects when they are given to certain animals. Among these is aspirin. Barbiturates, used as sleeping-drugs, penicillin, and several psychopharmaca drugs can cause birth defects in various animals. Even the administration of vitamin A and caffeine to some animals can cause birth defects, but as far as we know, none of these substances can cause birth defects in humans.

Considering the knowledge of the time, and what we know now about the difficulty of finding the right animal model, I think it would have been impossible to have predicted the risk of birth defects with Thalidomide.

But if Contergan hadn't been sold prescription-free in West Germany, thousands of children would certainly not have been born with birth defects. If Sweden and other countries had then possessed such a well-developed system for reporting side effects as we have today, then the deformities would certainly have been discovered earlier and the magnitude of the catastrophe would have been less tragic.

The Nerve Damage Should Have Been a Warning

Birth defects were not the only side effect of the "harmless" sleeping-drug Thalidomide. In November 1959 a German physician reported to Chemie-Grünenthal that two patients had received serious nerve damage, what are called polyneurites, after having taken Contergan over a period of time. But the company didn't take these reports of side effects seriously. The main reason was said to be that they were convinced of the drug's harmlessness and that polyneurites were not uncommon among older people. However, the company received more reports of nerve damage.

In December 1960 an article was published in the "British Medical Journal" suggesting that Thalidomide might cause polyneurites as well as numbness in the hands and feet, and painful cramps in the leg muscles.

Astra's Medical Department sent a copy of the British report to their representatives who visited doctors, asking them if Neurosedyn caused any of these side effects. Only one suspected case was reported.

In the Spring of 1961, there were 150 reports in West Germany where Contergan was suspected of causing polyneurites. Seventy-five more cases were reported in Britain.

To make some sense of it, Astra's Medical Director and Marketing Director visited Chemie-Grünenthal in June 1961. They were told that of the 150 cases, only a few were thought to have a connection with Thalidomide. In these cases, the patients had taken such high doses that they were considered to be abusing the drug.

Nevertheless, Astra decided to includ a warning about polyneurites in all information to physicians about Neurosedyn.

Even if it was probably hard to prove a connection between nerve damage and Contergan, the many reports from West Germany should have led to the drug being put on prescription, to prevent unrestricted sales to the public. Had this been done, many deformed children would have avoided such terrible handicaps.

We in Sweden should also have taken the warnings about polyneurites more seriously and reacted sooner. Adults injured by Neurosedyn also sued Astra which led to another settlement.

What Have We Learned?

The question that demands an answer the most is: Can we be sure that in the future, we won't face another tragedy like the Thalidomide disaster?

In order to prevent, as far as possible, a drug injuring foetuses, a number of safety tests are now carried out on different animals before a new drug can be tested on humans. In addition, as a rule, new drugs are not tested on women.

In Sweden, as in a number of other countries, no new drug may be tested on healthy people, or patients before the tests have been approved by both a supervisory agency and what is called an ethical committee. Such committees include physicians and laymen.

Before a new drug is approved (registered) by the authorities as a medicine which can be sold by pharmacies, a great many comprehensive safety tests are carried out. These include studies to evaluate the risk of damage to foetuses, cancer risks, possible genetic effects and how the new medicine behaves when taken together with other medicines.

An application for registration can encompass tens of thousands of pages of reports. Here the results of safety studies on different animals, tests of the effect on healthy people and their tolerance for the drug and clinical tests on patients are all given. When new drugs like metoprolol, felodipin, and omeprazol are concerned, they were tested on several thousand patients for a long period before they are approved for use.

The Damage Caused by the "Harmless" Diarrhoea Medicine

Ten years later the next drug related catastrophe happend. This time it wasn't a new drug that gave unexpectedly severe side effects. Tablets that had been used since the mid-30's to stop diarrhoea and prevent intestinal infections when travelling abroad were, in the early 70's, shown to cause severe nerve, muscle, and visual damage. The so-called SMON catastrophe was primarily a Japanese problem, but some cases were also discovered in Sweden and other countries.

Because of the increase in travel to warmer climates in the post-war era, it became more and more common for travellers to protect themselves from diarrhoea and other intestinal infections by taking Entero-vioform or Sterosan. The type of drug used in these medicines are called oxichinolines.

When I visited Mexico with a Swedish physician in 1962, we took Sterosan tablets as a preventative measure every day. Many of the other conference participants came down with annoying cases of diarrhoea. We thought we avoided this because of Sterosan's ability to kill bacteria. We had never heard of any side effects and didn't notice any. Now we know that the reason we were spared intestinal trouble was a combination of luck and our care in choosing what we ate and drank. There is in fact no evidence that this kind of drug actually prevents the intestinal infections which cause diarrhoea.

The Swedish paediatrician, Olle Hansson, was one of the first who suspected a connection between oxichinolines and visual problems. He had given an oxichinoline medication to a child who was suffering from a serious disease. At that time, during the 60's, there were no other medicines for that illness, which was thought to be fatal if the patient was not treated. When the boy began to suffer problems with his vision, Olle Hansson began to suspect that the oxichinoline was responsible. Occasional reports on side effects thought to arise in this kind of drug had begun to appear from other countries during the 60's.

Then, in the late 60's, a strange new disease began to spread in Japan. It was similar to the serious illness multiple sclerosis. The new disease was given the name SMON, an abbreviation of the Latin description: subacute myelo-optico-neuropathy. Before doctors realized that SMON was caused by a drug, they thought a new epidemic disease was responsible.

82

The Japanese government committee that was assigned to study the cause of the thousands of patients made invalid by SMON first worked under the hypothesis that the condition was caused by a new virus. When they finally realized that it was drugs of the type Enterovioform/Sterosan which caused the damage, these substances were banned in Japan on September 8, 1970. It was reported that there were then 186 products of this kind on the Japanese market.

That Japan was affected hardest of all by the SMON catastrophe is probably because of certain attitudes common to the Japanese, as well as the Japanese system of selling medicines through doctors instead of through pharmacies.

For Swedes and other Westerners, the heart is of central importance for health, well-being and emotions. For the Japanese, the stomach is a far more important organ than the heart. To understand how the SMON injuries were so widespread in Japan, it is important to realize that, for the Japanese, the stomach and the intestines are directly linked with well-being and feelings. At the slightest indication of problems from the stomach or intestines, the Japanese go to their doctors for help where they expect to receive some form of medication.

The many companies selling oxichinoline medications in Japan had convinced the doctors that these drugs were completely harmless. They claimed that they only had a local effect in the stomach and intestines. The Swiss company which discovered these substances thought it had evidence that they could not be absorbed from the intestine and therefore could not enter the bloodstream. They shouldn't be capable of damaging any organs in the body. So these drugs for the treatment of diarrhoea and other intestinal infections were regarded as completely harmless. They became very popular in Japan.

The fees Japanese doctors are allowed to charge their patients are far less than those paid to physicians in other industrialized countries. The main income of Japanese doctors came from selling medicines to patients in connection with consultations. As a rule, the doctor gives the patient a small bag with a two week supply of tablets. If a patient sought help for diarrhoea and was still sick two weeks later, the patient received a new bag of oxichinoline tablets, probably with a stronger dose. The stronger the dose and the longer the treatment, the more the doctor earned. In many cases, doctors ended up giving stronger and stronger doses of oxichinoline tablets to cure a disease caused by the tablets. The high doses and long treatments were probably the main reasons why so many patients were affected, and why the outbreak of SMON was so widespread in Japan.

In some twenty court cases, patients sued the Japanese authorities who had approved the drugs, and the pharmaceutical companies who had sold them. SMON patients sought damages together in class action suits. Even if there were a great many companies manufacturing and marketing oxichinoline products in Japan, the suits were primarily aimed at the large Swiss company Ciba-Geigy and two large Japanese companies. It had originally been Ciba and Geigy, who later merged into one company, who had developed these drugs. With the methods that were available when the drugs were first marketed fifty years ago, there was probably nothing to indicate that they were anything other than harmless. Suing the Japanese state was logical, since a state agency had approved the products and accepted the manufacturers' claims that they were harmless.

Olle Hansson's Struggle

The struggle fought by the patients and their lawyers during several years of legal action was very difficult. Olle Hansson was a witness in several trials. He was very upset about the suffering he had seen and the lack of will on the part of government agencies and the pharmaceutical companies to help the people who had suffered and been injured, often very severely. For several years Olle Hansson carried out an intensive campaign aimed at a complete ban on sales of oxichinoline products everywhere in the world.

In 1976 he wrote in the Swedish Medical Journal: "As long as my beak can squawk, I'll use every opportunity to spread information about SMON." He continued to fight until just before his death in May, 1985. Shortly before he died, he succeeded in convincing the chairman of Ciba-Geigy's Board of Directors to stop all sales of oxichinoline medications everywhere.

But a number of small local companies in the Third World undoubtedly continued to manufacture and sell oxichinolines. These companies could not be influenced by international public opinion.

The damages the Japanese government and the pharmaceutical

84

companies were forced to pay amounted to close to a billion dollars, one third from the government, the rest from the manufacturers.

It may seem strange that the struggle took so long and was so difficult. There were several reasons why the SMON catastrophe was harder to deal with than the Thalidomide disaster.

There was one similarity between the Thalidomide and SMON tragedies. In both cases the drugs that had caused the damage were believed to be completely harmless. Scientists were convinced that Thalidomide could not be transferred from a mother to her foetus. They refused to believe the reports of birth defects. When SMON damage was reported, scientists and company management refused to believe that the injuries could have been caused by the company's product because they were sure they had proved that the drug couldn't be absorbed and thereby not cause any damage.

When it was firmly established that oxichinolines were responsible for SMON, questions began to be asked about the drug's alleged medical effect. It was discovered that there was no real evidence that these medications could cure or prevent diarrhoea. Since the drugs lacked a demonstrable effect, and under some conditions could result in very serious side effects, it was obvious that they should be withdrawn from the market everywhere.

However, it was several years before this happened. One reason was that governments and doctors in India and other developing countries in the tropics thought they needed these drugs to treat parasites and other infections in the intestines.

When I contacted several government agencies in India in October 1977 to see if it would be possible for Astra to work together with an Indian company in order to establish a modern Western-style pharmaceutical company in the country, I was confronted with a rather interesting criticism of Swedish efforts to ban oxichinoline products.

Dr. Gothoskar, who was responsible for government supervision of drugs in India, was obviously irritated. He suddenly interrupted our conversation and asked: "Why are you Swedes interfering with how we deal with drug questions in India?"

I was confused by this, and asked what he meant?

A member of the Indian parliament had read in the chamber a quote from a Swedish newspaper in which a Dr. Hansson had criticised the Indian authorities for continuing to allow sales of oxikinoline products in India. When Dr. Gothoskar answered his critic in parliament, he had said:

"We need these drugs to treat amoebic dysentery and other parasitic diseases. Our own experts have concluded that the available alternative medicines have other side effects which can be just as serious as those caused by oxichinolines. Those other products are also more expensive. That's why we want to continue to use oxichinolines."

When he finished describing the debate in parliament, he raised his voice: "You can hardly be familiar with the situation in India and the special problems we face here."

When you try to understand, which is not the same as accepting, Ciba-Geigy's late withdrawal of oxichinoline products from developing countries, you have to remember that the authorities in these countries saw a need for these drugs to treat tropical diseases. It's natural that the company lawyers and management were strongly influenced by the decisions of the governments involved. The World Health Organization's position must have been decisive as well. For several years after oxichinolines were forbidden in Japan in 1970, these drugs were still on the WHO list of important medicines for developing countries. From a Swedish point of view this seemed very strange. Olle Hansson's campaign led to removing the drugs from the list, and finally to a total ban on sales.

As the representative for Ciba-Geigy in Sweden for most of the 70's, we at Hässle were greatly affected by the SMON debate, even if we weren't directly involved. We had also co-operated with Ciba-Geigy scientists in Basel on a special research project during that period. In the course of informal discussions, off the record, our researchers were often critical of Ciba-Geigy's continued sales of oxichinoline products. We also tried, in other ways to influence Ciba-Geigy by communicating the positions of Swedish doctors on the issue.

There's no doubt that it was mainly Olle Hansson's stubborn efforts that were responsible, but the criticism of other physicians also contributed to Ciba-Geigy's decision to stop all sales of these drugs in March 1985. Olle Hansson's long struggle is described in the book *Ciba-Geigy bakom fasaden (Ciba-Geigy: Behind the Facade)*, which was published in Sweden in 1989, more than four years after his death.

People who have had contact with the company since then have confirmed that Ciba-Geigy has taken steps to prevent similar tragedies in the future.

A working group comprising various specialists from the company is now responsible, more effectively than before, for continuously monitoring their drugs, and making risk evaluations. Such questions are now openly discussed with outside specialists at annual conferences where representatives from the responsible government agencies also participate.

Just as the Thalidomide disaster of the 60's was a turning point for the pharmaceutical industry leading to improved safety studies of new drugs before they could be tested on humans and introduced to the health care system, the SMON tragedy was an alarm clock that woke doctors, governments and pharmaceutical companies to the importance of paying attention to all reports of side effects from drugs. It is also now understood that even older, established products have to be continually re-evaluated. The risk of possible side effects must be weighed against the demonstrable medical value of the drug.

Can We Survive?

The stricter controls on drugs that followed the Thalidomide disaster required increased resources. Astra's central laboratories for drug safety developed new methods for evaluating the risk of foetal defects, in an expansive operation.

In order to live up to new demands for a better understanding of the effects and active mechanisms of drugs, Hässle also needed to considerably increase its resources. We also required additional qualified staff in areas such as biochemistry and bioanalytical chemistry.

During the early 60's, we became more and more convinced that we could not survive in the long run with the goal we had set up – to develop products primarily for the Swedish market. We agreed, within the Hässle management group, that we had to create new products capable of competing internationally and which would also have to meet the strict registration standards introduced in many countries after the Thalidomide disaster.

There was another reason why we needed newer and larger premises.

Most of our personnel worked in our old premises in Gothenburg. But since 1960, a dozen researchers and technicians had been working in laboratories we had built in the suburb of Mölndal. The distance between the two locations made it difficult to co-ordinate their work. To create the feeling of a unified company working towards a common goal, we urgently needed to bring together the entire workforce in suitable premises.

When Hässle presented a proposal costing twenty-three million kronor (around three million USD) to build new offices and laboratories in Mölndal in the Spring of 1964, most of Astra's group management was sceptical. Only Group president Arne Wegerfelt and his colleague Sven Sundling supported us.

It is easy to understand why the Group's Board was doubtful about this major investment. Three million dollars was at that point more than Hässle's total annual sales. In 1967, there were seven research and development organizations within Astra. Their results were hardly encouraging.

The largest research effort had been made at the central laboratory in Södertälje. In the decades between Astra's successful marketing of lidocain in 1948 and 1964, not a single important product had been developed by any of the Group's research and development departments.

Astra's subsidiary in the United States had comparable resources to those at Hässle. Two other Swedish subsidiaries, Draco and Tika, were smaller than Hässle, but their close proximity to universities indicated that Astra planned to expand their research and development departments to insure that they would have adequate resources.

The research laboratories at the Group's subsidiaries in Britain and France lacked both the resources and the qualified personnel to develop modern medicines.

Astra's Board met at Hässle for the first time ever in September, 1964. The decision was to be made on our request to build new premises as well as to employ more researchers and technicians. A "no" would have been seen by us as meaning that the board didn't believe in our hopes for growth. We wouldn't be able to employ the people we needed to carry out our projects. There was a risk that several of our most important researchers might lose confidence in the company and leave us.

I arrived outside the room where the meeting was to take place at the time scheduled for my presentation of our projects, but the board meeting was running late, and during the hour I sat waiting to be called in, I felt the destiny of our company hanging over my head. The future depended on whether my presentation of our projects would convince the board of their validity.

Unfortunately, I couldn't point to any marketable products as result of our research. Instead, all I could do was present the projects we hoped would be successful within a few years. After my presentation, the Chairman of the Board, Jacob Wallenberg, said:

"There's nothing wrong with his enthusiasm! But it remains to be seen if there is any realism in what he is saying."

As Wallenberg spoke with the other members of the board, the indications were clear - the chairman didn't believe in our projects. Jacob Wallenberg was something of a legend in Swedish business circles. He had been the chairman of dozens of companies. He had certainly listened to countless Research Directors and Technical Directors glowingly present projects that had later failed to deliver what they promised. I was close to panic as the risk our proposal would be rejected loomed larger. In a desperate attempt to save the situation I said:

"I understand completely why the Board is sceptical about our ability to develop products that would make such a large investment profitable. Nevertheless, we have proof that an American company thinks our research is worthwhile. When I was in the United States a couple of months ago, we were given a check for 50,000 dollars from Dow Chemicals for the right to study a product we had patented. That was a major addition to our research budget, a quarter of a million kronor."

The first stage in Mölndal was finished in 1960. The pharmacology laboratory with the animal department and a pilot facility for chemical synthesis can be seen.

The Chairman interrupted:

"He doesn't have to teach me exchange rates. Did he say that Dow gave Hässle 50,000 dollars for a product? The people at Dow are my friends."

The Chairman took a piece of paper out of his suit pocket and wrote down: "Hässle 50,000 dollars Dow". While he stuck the paper back in his pocket, the Group president indicated that I should leave the room. It was difficult to go without hearing the final decision.

That evening as I tried to analyse my mistakes, I realized that I should have presented our research and development work in a different way: I should have started by admitting that we hadn't succeeded in any of the six projects we began after March, 1959, when we started our biological-chemical research. Then I should have outlined the new principles we were guided by, thanks to the advice we had received from our consultants at the University of Gothenburg. I should have explained the difference between the research we had carried out earlier and the new strategy that Arvid Carlsson had outlined which led us later to the medicines alprenolol and metoprolol.

Despite my pessimism, the next morning Sven-Arne Norlindh announced that the board had approved our proposal. The Group's president, Arne Wegerfelt, had given us his strong support. However, the Chairman of the Board was still doubtful. After dinner Jacob Wallenberg had said:

"This was an expensive dinner. It cost twenty-three million kronor."

I never found out if the check from Dow had affected the decision.

When I spoke with Sven Sundling in 1981 and mentioned how I felt about the meeting with Jacob Wallenberg, Sven told me how concerned the Chairman of the Board was about the company's long-term growth:

"During all the years that I, as secretary to the Board, had the opportunity to study Jacob Wallenberg's way of directing its work, I never failed to be impressed by his strong desire to support research and insure the company's long-term development. Despite his own major holdings in Astra stocks, he never showed any interest in giving larger dividends to the shareholders. To the greatest possible degree, he wanted the company's profits to be used for long-term investments."

IV. Setbacks and Successes

It was naive to start six research projects during the same period as we did in 1959 and 1960. None of these projects resulted in any usable drugs. We didn't realize then the extent of the resources required for creating worthwhile medicines. Nevertheless, it wasn't just the lack of resources that prevented our projects from reaching the goals we had set.

We also lacked experience in the complicated research necessary to find new medicines. And above all, we lacked qualified personnel in the biological and medical sciences.

Experienced consultants within the fields of physiology and medicine gave us valuable advice. But without qualified personnel of our own we couldn't even ask the right questions. We had no way to follow the advice we received on a daily basis in our working routines since we lacked experienced pharmacologists for our animal experiments.

A young physician, Lars Garberg, made admirable contributions when he planned and equipped our pharmacological laboratory and our facility for animal experiments. Aside from the six months he had spent at the University of Bonn, he had hardly any opportunities to broaden his knowledge of industrial pharmacology before he was forced to take responsibility for testing and evaluating the new compounds that our chemists were producing at a rapid rate.

In one project, we tried to create new medicines by isolating the active substances in tropical plants used in traditional medicine. Unfortunately, we lacked the methods available to scientists today to isolate active substances in plants and determine their chemical structures. The story of how we were forced to abandon this promising research is told in the chapter "Medicines from the Plant Kingdom".

The other five projects which didn't succeed were run by chemists. According to the then-traditional approach to pharmaceutical research, we synthesized a number of chemical compounds in each project. These were tested with different screening methods, looking for medicines to combat different diseases. Experience has shown that this type of chemical-biological research requires the synthesis of thousands of substances in order to find a single usable drug. Unfortunately, we didn't have the resources for that kind of research.

The three projects that were started in 1961, and in the years that followed, worked from the new biological principles that are described in the chapter: "A New Road Toward the Goal".

In one project, a very promising medicine was created which was marketed internationally. However, despite reassuring safety trials and clinical studies on several thousand patients, unexpected side effects were discovered in a few patients after marketing. As a result, the drug was withdrawn from the market eighteen months after its introduction.

Two other projects were very successful.

In the chapter: "Medicines for the Heart and Blood Pressure" the development of modern drugs for heart diseases are described. One of these drugs has been used over a period of many years by more than twelve million patients.

The chapter: "Peptic Ulcer Drugs" tells the story of the discovery of a new principle for the treatment of ulcers in the stomach and the small intestine as well as the oesophagus. After more than twenty years of difficult work, a drug was developed which has been used in the treatment of more than one hundred million patients all over the world.

Medicines from the Plant Kingdom

Our company's biggest selling product in 1954 was called Adocardin comp. This remedy contained an extract of the herb *Adonis vernalis*. The catalogue that was sent to physicians described in a very convincing manner the extract's positive effect on various heart complaints.

Adonis extract was supposed to have a similar effect as digitalis on the heart, but was supposed to be far more gentle. Digitalis, which was originally extracted from foxglove leaves, often had side effects. With Adonis extract, doctors had a remedy that according to our catalogue could be used for mild heart problems without the risk of side effects.

In May 1954, the Royal Medical Board asked us to prove the claimed effect of Adonis extract on the heart. If we couldn't demonstrate an acceptable effect by a certain date, the preparation would have to be withdrawn from the market. Since a large portion of the company's profits came from this remedy, it was an embarrassing situation.

I sought help from Finn Sandberg, who was a professor of Pharmacognosy, the study of medicinal plants. Professor Sandberg had succeeded in isolating and determining the chemical structure of a number of medicinal plants. He had also studied their biological effects.

Finn Sandberg's colleague, Lars Garberg, was assigned to develop an experimental method on animals to try to document the effect of the adonis extract on the heart.

After three months, Garberg succeeded in producing data that was accepted by the Royal Medical Board. Our most important remedy was saved, and survived for more than a decade. But then both our own requirements, as well as those of the Medical Board, for the documentation of the medical value of drugs became more strict. We couldn't adequately demonstrate the clinical value of Adocardin in a way that could meet the new standards, so the remedy was deregistered.

There was still interest within the company for active medicinal substances from plants. Finn Sandberg got me interested in studying tropical plants in the hope of finding completely new kinds of medicines. On expeditions to the tropical areas of Africa, Central America, and Asia he had collected plants which had been used in traditional medicine. Back at the University of Uppsala, Professor Sandberg made extracts of these plants looking for active substances by studying possible effects on animals.

Professor Sandberg said that we should learn from the experience of traditional medicine through contacts with village medicine men. He pointed to the many medicines that had their origin in the plant kingdom. The largest number of species are found in the tropics. In a warm climate, plants also produce more chemical substances than they do in our colder climate so there were several reasons to look in the tropics for interesting medicinal plants.

After Finn Sandberg talked us into concentrating on phytochemical research, that is, looking for medicines from the plant kingdom, we received a letter from a missionary in the French Congo. The missionary's wife asked us to send medicine for the mission's infirmary. She was a university-trained botanist and was interested in the plants used by medicine men to treat illnesses. She had taken notes of the medicine men's descriptions of the effects of their remedies.

On the advice of Finn Sandberg, we asked her for samples of herbs, leaves, bark and roots from different plants along with descriptions of the diseases for which these remedies were used.

It turned out to be almost impossible to draw any conclusions about the medical effects. The information from the medicine men offered us little help. Their explanations of the cause of the symptoms of different ailments were far too vague. Far too often the medicinal plants were used in connection with spells or religious rites. Some of the plants were used as sexual stimulants. Some were supposed to cure mental illnesses.

At the University of Uppsala, these herbs and other plant residues were turned into extracts which were tested on mice and rats. We looked for effects to justify going ahead and isolating the active substances and the determination of chemical structures. We hoped that this work would lead to new medicines.

Altogether, we studied around seventy herbs and other plant residues without finding anything worth following up. My feeling was that the active substances in most of the extracts were poisonous.

When we reappraised the projects we were working on in early 1961, we found it impossible to continue with phytochemical research. According to the minutes from a meeting in February, 1961, Lennart Sölvell maintained that it was highly improbable that we would find anything of interest in the limited number of plant extracts we were able to study.

Our chemists underlined that looking for completely new structures in plants was of great interest to the chemists. Nature has an incredible ability to create highly complicated chemical substances. But for this kind of research to be meaningful, you have to be able to determine the chemical structures of the active substances in the plants. We didn't have the resources to do this.

There was another strong reason behind our decision to discontinue the project. We couldn't afford to work with research projects where we couldn't learn anything from our mistakes.

In biological-chemical research you can often find a connection between chemical structure and biological effects. Even the synthesis of new substances that don't lead to medicines can provide direction for future work. But after we had tested some seventy plant extracts in the phytochemical project, we hadn't learned anything that indicated what plants we ought to study as our work continued.

In successful projects, a new medicine could be created after several hundred chemical compounds were synthesized and tested on isolated organs and animals. But even if we tested hundreds of herbs without positive results, we still wouldn't have any idea where we should continue to look.

Twenty years after we decided to discontinue the research aimed at finding medicines in tropical plants, Lennart Sölvell and I found confirmation that our decision had been right.

During a trip in Southeast Asia, we met a Swede in Thailand who had devoted more than ten years to supporting such research projects in several developing countries. Travelling across the region for more than a decade, he had handed out millions of dollars to various projects in the hope of finding useful medicinal plants which could create export industries for those countries. The hope was to find valuable medicines by studying traditional medicine.

When the Swedish researcher told us about the projects he was working with, we couldn't resist asking him about the results. What had all the invested millions produced after all those years?

After a moment's thought he was forced to admit that there was scarcely anything positive to talk about. The only interesting discovery seemed to be that a frequently used laxative had been shown to be poisonous. Now people were being encouraged to stop using the remedy. No plants had been found that could provide valuable medicines. Despite this, he didn't seem to have any plans to abandon the work.

Because of the great interest in natural products and alternative medicine, people often ask if medicines with demonstrable effect can't be found in the plant kingdom? In January 1989, to learn how phytochemical research is carried out with more modern methods than we had in the 1960's, I visited Professor Gunnar Samuelsson at the University of Uppsala. He had succeeded Finn Sandberg as Professor of Pharmacognosy. In a short paper, he summarized his views on how we should work today to develop medicines from tropical plants:

"Hässle's unsuccessful experiences trying to develop medicines from tropical medicinal plants in the 1960's are not unique. When pharmaceutical researchers in the early 50's succeeded in isolating the blood pressure-reducing alkaloid reserpin from the Indian medicinal plant *Rauwolfia serpentina*, many pharmaceutical companies were greatly interested in looking for medicines in medicinal plants. Despite the spending of much money and labour to such projects, there were no apparent results. The main reason seems to have been that there were no methods for quickly and reliably testing the extracts that were taken from these plants. Another was that the medicine men's descriptions of the use of and effects of medicinal plants failed to provide any evidence for medical effects. So there wasn't enough direction to help work out biological test methods to study the extracts from these plants.

"The main problem in looking for plants that can act against a particular illness is to find suitable methods for studying the medical effects. A plant contains many different substances. There may be several hundred components, of which perhaps just a few or even only one carries the effect you're looking for. For that reason, the extract you make from the plant is a complicated combination in which the biologically active substances are usually found in very small quantities.

"To find out if a plant extract could be interesting pharmaceutically, you have to be able to test it for the effect you're looking for. You also have to be able to isolate and test the active substance that you think gives the effect. The greatest difficulty is to be able to find substances with specific effects in a sufficiently simple way. The methods most often used in studies of medicinal plants don't give sufficient guidance in finding usable drugs.

"While the research into medicinal plants produces little in the form of new medicines that affect specific organs, we have been far more successful with bacteria and other microorganisms. Penicillin and other valuable antibiotics are the result of this research.

"The quest for antibiotics in fungi and other microorganisms is similar to the hunt for pharmacologically active substances in medicinal plants. In both cases the goal is to take small quantities of active substances from a naturally occurring product. When looking for antibiotics, it is often easy to test the effect. Testing how an antibiotic kills or impedes the growth of bacteria can be done quickly. It is much harder and is more time consuming to test an extract for its medical effect on a particular illness.

"In order to reach better results when studying medicinal plants, our department has begun working with physicians in Somalia. The African doctor we work with is currently being trained in clinical pharmacology at Stockholm's Huddinge Hospital. When his training is over, he'll return to Somalia to work with some of his country's medicine men in studying some of the plants that are traditionally used as medicines. The physician will make a diagnosis of the patients who are treated by the medicine men. He will then follow the patients during and after their treatment in order to see if the remedy has any effect. The plants that are judged to be of interest will be studied here at our department. We're working on developing better testing methods to investigate the extracts from these medicinal plants.

"There are around 250,000 species of plants on the Earth. Only a handful, perhaps 6 or 7 percent, have been studied from a chemical and pharmacological point of view. Several valuable medicines have been developed as a result of the investigation of medicinal plants based on old traditions. These include morphine and papverine from the opium-poppy, digitoxin from the leaves of the foxglove, quinine and quinidine from cinchona bark, and atropine from belladonna leaves. There are probably many more valuable medicines in the hundreds of thousands of plants that have still not been studied."

New Discoveries

Gunnar Samuelsson's project is now to study medicinal plants from Somalia in the hope of finding medicines for treating diarrhoea and to combat inflammation. As an example of the interesting discoveries that have recently been made at other institutions, he refers to a Chinese researcher who has found a remedy to treat the most resistant form of malaria which cannot be treated with the current synthetic malaria drugs. This remedy comes from the plant *Artemisia annua*, which is related to sagebrush and wormwood.

Messengers of the Brain

In their book from 1988 *Hjärnans budbärare (Messengers of the Brain)*, pharmacologist Arvid Carlsson and science writer Lena Carlsson write about mental illness. They describe the causes of diseases of the mind and the treatment of mental disorders in the past and today. They also take up what may be possible in the future. I've taken the title of his chapter from their book.

Before the 1950's, little was known about how the brain worked. It is without doubt the most complicated organ in the body. So it's not surprising that the development of psychopharmaca took much longer than that of medicines for physical ailments. It has been much more difficult to determine the working mechanism behind psycho-drugs. No one knew before the mechanism of communication between the cells of the brain. Thanks to the intensive research of the last thirty years, the neurotransmitters or signal substances, the "messengers", which transfer information between the brain's cells and to our consciousness have been discovered.

Mental disturbances such as schizophrenia and manic excitation are probably caused by overly-powerful impulses from the signal substances. Yet, if the signals are too weak, depression can result.

Research carried out at Arvid Carlsson's Department of Pharmacy at the University of Gothenburg has added much to what we know about these signal substances in the brain.

In 1961, Hans Corrodi and Arvid Carlsson began what was to be a decade of very constructive co-operation. A number of interesting pieces of the puzzle were found which contributed to the picture we

101

now have of the functions of the brain. Hans Corrodi's work was pure basic research which he carried out alongside the goal-oriented projects he was working with at Hässle.

Basic Research

This basic research was carried out between 1961 and 1965 in the hope of producing substances which could retard the breakdown of the neurotransmitters adrenaline and noradrenaline (norepinephrine) in the brain. Some of the substances that were synthesized showed interesting effects during the animal trials.

We were sure that one substance, H22/54, which was created in 1962, would become an important scientific tool. There was also some hope that it could be developed into a medicine. It was tested on humans after it had passed our safety trials. When it turned out that the effect of H22/54 on humans was too short-term to be of use, we stopped working with it. The fruitless work with this substance illustrates one of the many problems we had to cope with in pharmaceutical research.

For studies on mice, very small quantities of H22/54 were required. To produce the substance, chemists had to synthesize twelve intermediate steps. This meant that they had to produce twelve completely new chemical compounds, each of which often demanded difficult-to-master syntheses.

When H22/54 was to undergo safety trials and human tests, kilogram-sized quantities were required. It was obvious that the system of producing twelve intermediate products would be too expensive. If H22/54 was to be more than just an interesting tool in basic research, if it was to be used one day as a medicine to control some mental disturbance, it was urgent that we find a simpler way to synthesize it. Otherwise the drug would be far too expensive.

After three year's work, the chemists succeeded in developing a manufacturing process that required only five steps. But just as we were celebrating that accomplishment, we discovered that the effect of H22/54 on humans was too short. So we abandoned the project.

After several more years of basic research, Arvid Carlsson's conclusion was that so many interesting discoveries had been made that a goal-oriented project should be able to build on the work to develop medicines for treating some mental illnesses.

Mental Illnesses

Mental illnesses affect many people and cause considerable suffering.

Like heart disease, depression is a common sickness. According to estimates, 30 percent of women and 15 percent of men will suffer from depression sometime in their lifetime. This condition differs from ordinary low-spiritedness, or "blues". A person suffering from depression cannot be cheered up with the methods that usually work with someone who is just feeling a little low.

The typical symptoms are extreme low-spiritedness, listlessness and fatigue. The patients can sit and stare straight ahead for long periods without being able to do anything. A common symptom of depression is that the person wakes up earlier than usual in the morning with strong feelings of anxiety.

In some patients, the periods of depression alternate with manic periods characterized by powerful feelings of exhilaration and exaggerated activity. These patients are called manic-depressive.

We probably don't know how common such manias are, as they aren't brought to the attention of doctors as often as depression. In the manic phase, the patient often feels very happy and certainly not ill. Only those around him or her notice the overly intensive activity.

Schizophrenia and other so-called psychoses affect around two percent of the Swedish population. Psychoses are often characterized by hallucinations and delusions.

Senile dementia is a disease of old age and has become a growing social problem. The symptoms are deteriorating memory and occasional confusion. The reason is believed to be the death of nerve cells leading to a deficiency in signal substances. But no one knows what causes this.

In the case of depression, mania and schizophrenia, scientists believe that the signal substances of the brain, the "messengers", are out of balance. There may be many reasons for this. Genetic factors as well as social and other external factors may be involved.

Mental illness is treated with drugs which work on the signal system in different ways. Side effects are often a problem, so better drugs are needed that are both more effective and more selective in their effect.

There is no effective medicine today for senile dementia. Current research is looking at finding drugs that can compensate for the shortage of signal substances.

In order to reach the best possible result when treating mental disease, physicians are aware that patients need more than just drugs. It is extremely important that they also receive psychological and social support and be stimulated to activity.

Depression, Mania, and Parkinson's Disease

The results of the research carried out at Arvid Carlsson's department during the 1960's indicated that we could start goal-oriented projects to develop medicines for both depression and mania as well as for the disturbance in the brain that leads to Parkinson's disease.

In 1962 and 1963, there were attempts to treat patients who were so severely disabled with Parkinson's Disease that they couldn't move their arms. The drug L-dopa had demonstrated such interesting effects on animals that it was considered worth testing.

When a solution of L-dopa was injected into a severely handicapped patient, the effect was quite dramatic. She could suddenly move her hands and arms. She could even eat by herself, but there were severe side effects so the project was discontinued.

A similar study, carried out in the United States, revealed that patients could endure the drug if L-dopa is initially administered in very small doses that are gradually increased until the desired effect is reached.

Today, L-dopa and variants of the drug provide immeasureable relief to Parkinson's patients.

For the treatment of manias, Arvid Carlsson suggested that we should try to develop substances that would affect the neurotransmitter dopamine. Unfortunately, we didn't have the resources for such a project. It was taken over in the early 70's by Astra's main research unit which worked with Arvid Carlsson.

During 1968 Arvid Carlsson, Hans Corrodi and I agreed to concentrate our resources on a project to find a drug to fight depression. This was primarily carried out within the framework of our grant to Arvid Carlsson's university department along with our own exploratory research.

Medicines Against Depression

At the time, it was thought that anti-depressive drugs worked because they strengthened the effect of the neurotransmitter noradrenaline on the brain. But Arvid Carlsson thought that there was a good possibility that the neurotransmitter serotonin played an important role in the origin of depression. He coined the phrase "the serotonin hypothesis" for its anti-depressive effect and suggested that we develop a drug to strengthen the serotonin effect on the brain.

Such a drug could be expected to help those patients who were not helped by existing medicines. Those drugs mainly strengthened the effect of noradrenaline. There were other reasons for starting a project to find a new medicine against depression. Most of the then-current drugs caused disturbing side effects the most serious of which was damage to the heart when very high doses had been administered in attempted suicides. Victims actually died from the effect of the antidepressant. One of the goals of our project was to create a new drug without these extremely harmful side effects.

Another disadvantage of the antidepressants at that time was that they affected the cell receptors for the neurotransmitter acetylcholine. This meant that patients suffered from palpitations of the heart. Their mouths became dry which often resulted in damage to their teeth, especially among older patients. They experienced problems with their vision. Men with prostrate complaints often had greater problems urinating. By searching for a drug that wouldn't affect the acetylcholine receptors we hoped to avoid these side effects.

To test the theory about the importance of serotonin, Arvid Carlsson and Hans Corrodi began to look for a drug that might have an effect on serotonin. Animal tests revealed that the drug chlorimipramine from the Swiss company Geigy greatly affected serotonin as well as noradrenaline. When Arvid Carlsson contacted Geigy's researchers, it turned out that they didn't know about the effect on serotonin. They also didn't think it was worth discussing. At that time Geigy was more interested in another antidepressant which they wanted to market.

Eventually, however, their interest in chlorimipramine revived, and they marketed it as an antidepressant under the name Anafranil.

We were looking for a drug that only affected serotonin. Animal tests found such an effect in a drug that had been used for a long time to treat allergies. While the drug itself didn't meet our project goals, its chemical structure became the starting point for a synthesis program. Hans Corrodi produced a number of substances that were variants of the allergy drug.

In 1969, we synthesized the compound H102/09. Animal tests indicated that it met all the requirements of our project goals. We applied for a patent.

After the approved safety tests, we quickly carried out the trials on healthy people that are required before the authorities grant permission for clinical tests. We employed a clinical pharmacologist to lead the clinical trials. We were very optimistic. This project, we thought, would soon give us our second original product, following the heart medicine alprenolol which had been approved for marketing in 1967.

One day in the Spring of 1971, Astra's president Arne Wegerfeldt and his vice president, Hans-Erik Leufstedt, came to our offices in Mölndal on urgent business. When I was called in to the guest dining room a few hours later, I discovered that they had talked Hans Corrodi into moving to Astra's main headquarters in Södertälje, outside of Stockholm. As Research Director, he would co-ordinate the Group's research and product development. It had also been decided that Corrodi would take with him the psychopharmaca project and the compound H102/09.

The reason for moving the project from Hässle was the Group management's belief that we'd already had too many projects for the limited resources at our disposal. But had the company, at that time, given us a little more money, we would have been in a good position to carry the project all the way through to the finished medicine.

The project and H102/09 were transferred to Astra in January, 1972. Contact with Arvid Carlsson wasn't as close as it had been. When Hans Corrodi tragically died just over a year later, the strong personal relationship between Arvid Carlsson and the researchers in Södertälje weakened.

After more than 10 years of safety tests on different animals, and clinical studies in several countries, H102/09, or zemilidin as it was called, was approved in 1982 as a drug in Sweden and several other countries.

Many patients, who had previously not been helped by anti-depressants, were liberated from their condition thanks to zemilidin. Patients who had found it difficult to undergo treatment because of the side effects of previous drugs, had no such problems with zemilidin. The drug had indeed met our expectations.

The head of the Group, Ulf Widengren, had great hopes for zemilidin since the drug could be tolerated so well. He thought that zemilidin would be a big international success for the company.

But when more than 200,000 patients had used zemilidin, a few reports appeared of occasional side effects in the form of paralysis. Since only one of the thousand patients who took part in the controlled clinical tests had shown the same symptoms, it was difficult to believe that they were caused by zemilidin. But when more cases were reported, and were deemed to be serious, zemilidin was withdrawn from the international market.

This was a very difficult decision. When it was decided to remove zemilidin from the market, on September 17, 1983, nearly 80,000 patients in Sweden alone had used the drug. Many of them were patients who had not responded well to other medicines. There was a considerable risk that their depression would return. Some might even take their own lives as a result. However, in Sweden, doctors could continue to prescribe zemilidin under what was called a personal licence procedure.

The main reason that zemilidin was withdrawn from sales everywhere was that there was no scientific explanation for the unusual side effects that had been reported. It was felt at that time that we were unable to offer physicians any guidance as to which patients might be susceptible to the side effects.

The neurological side effects that were reported are called the Guillain-Barré Syndrome. This involves nerve damage that can cause muscular paralysis. Such symptoms had previously been reported in cases when zemilidin was not administered. The estimate is that one person in 50,000 shows these symptoms. When there were indications of an increase in 1983, a warning was sent to doctors to monitor possible side effects from the new medicine. Up until the withdrawal from the market on September 17, 1983, 8 cases had been reported in Sweden. Since at most, 80,000 patients had used zemilidin, that means a frequency of at least one in 10,000, compared to one in 50,000 among non-users.

This may show how difficult it was for Astra's management and for the Swedish authorities to decide to withdraw a medicine that had been of great help to many patients suffering from severe depression. No one has ever suggested that this difficult decision was affected by economic considerations.

Many physicians and thousands of patients felt upset and betrayed. They hadn't experienced any side effects outside Sweden, it was difficult to understand the decision. In countries that lacked the system for reporting side effects that is used in Sweden, no one had heard of any side effects.

Several newspaper articles said Astra's quick decision had created respect and goodwill for the company.

The first scientist to test zemilidin clinically was Professor Jan Wålinder, Head Physician at the Psychiatric Clinic in the University Hospital of Linköping. In June 1989 I asked for his opinion of the drug and its withdrawal from the market.

Jan Wålinder thought that zemilidin was a very worthwhile drug, especially for cases of depression in which no other medicine helped. The Swedish authorities still licence doctors to prescribe zemilidin for such cases, even though the drug is not registered. But in most other countries it is not possible to obtain zemilidin even under licence.

Jan Wålinder maintained that he is not worried about the serious, but rare, side effects experienced with zemilidin. If the doctor watches for symptoms of over-sensitivity to the drug, Wålinder says, there's no risk. The few patients who show such symptoms can stop the treatment. If no symptoms are discovered during the first four weeks, the physician can continue the treatment without worry. Jan Wålinder didn't think zemilidin should have been withdrawn, because he thought, there was a need for it.

As far as the marketing of the drug was concerned, Jan Wålinder thought that Astra should have been more careful by initially only letting hospital psychiatrists use it until more experience had been gained. He didn't think a fixed dose should have been recommended, but rather a more flexible approach. Arvid Carlsson says that he, at an early stage, had in fact recommended a lower dose, especially for older patients.

Lars Werkö was responsible for research and medical questions within Astra when zemilidin was tested and marketed. His comments in the pharmaceutical industry trade journal "Arena" may be of interest:

"It is possible that a longer observation period when zemilidin was introduced could have meant that the number of severe neurological side effects would have been reduced giving better opportunities to modify the dosage recommendations."

By applying the "warning guide" recommended by Jan Wålinder, the company could probably have avoided complete withdrawal from the market.

It's easy to say afterwards what could have been done, but this shows how difficult it can be to make a decision when reports of side effects appear, and how seriously the pharmaceutical industry and the regulatory authorities have to take these concerns.

Fortunately, it is unusual that side effects are discovered after so many patients have used a drug. It was particularly tragic in this case, since so many people suffering from severe depression could only be helped with zemilidin.

The set-back was a great disappointment to the researchers who worked for fourteen years on the project. It was also felt by the company which spent around 50 million dollars on research, safety studies and clinical tests.

The set-back with zemildin had no serious long-term effect on Astra's economic growth. There were other valuable drugs being developed. Instead it had a different, and just as serious, effect. Astra's president, Ulf Widengren, became wary of continued pharmaceutical research of the kind that had led to zemilidin.

Nevertheless, it was the hope that zemilidin would result in considerably less side effects and would be safer than other anti-depressants that had largely motivated the effort. Ulf Widengren didn't know if he could rely in the future on the assurances of researchers that a new drug was safe. He began to discuss the possibility of concentrating on generic medicines, already well-established base drugs (for which the patent protection had expired, also called "standard drugs").

In the summer of 1986, the heads of Astra's subsidiaries, research directors, medical advisors and marketing directors were called to a special conference. There was nothing on the agenda about the two new products we expected to register shortly, the blood pressure medicine felodipin and the ulcer medicine omeprazol. Instead, generic drugs and even prescription-free medicines were discussed as options for Astra's concentration. Fortunately, however, the company continued to concentrate on long-term research aimed at developing new products.

Had Astra concentrated on standard drugs instead of patent-protected pharmaceuticals developed with its own research, it would certainly have been impossible to keep the 1,500 researchers and technicians working for the company's Swedish research and development organizations. Since only unique products can establish themselves in the long run in hard international competition, Astra's potential for continued development would certainly have been limited if the decision had been made to give priority to standard drugs over the company's own patented orginal products.

One question that interested many people after the withdrawal of zemilidin from the market was if the researchers could produce a new and safer drug with the same effective working mechanism as zemilidin. I asked Arvid Carlsson that question in December 1988.

He answered that he had long thought about the problem. He had suggested that Astra work on a new drug with the same biological effect as zemilidin several times, but with a somewhat altered chemical structure. In zemilidin, there is a double bond between two carbon atoms. This could have been the source of the side effects. Arvid commented:

"Unfortunately, I was unable to interest Astra's researchers in such a project. It seemed as if they had completely lost interest in developing a new drug to fight depression."

Arvid Carlsson pointed to the interest other pharmaceutical companies had shown in his "serotin-hypothesis", which lay behind the development of zemilidin. In March, 1990 it was reported that the American company, Eli Lilly, estimated that their anti-depressant Prozac would reach sales of USD 500 million that year. The drug's success was said to be because of its unique characteristics. According to Arvid Carlsson, Prozac is based on the principles he outlined when zemilidin was developed.

Medicines for the Heart and Blood Pressure

The first result of our biological-chemical research was alprenolol. This medicine was approved for the treatment of some heart ailments by the Swedish authorities in October, 1967 and was followed by approval in many other countries. A few years later, we were able to demonstrate that alprenolol also reduces blood pressure and is a very useful drug for the treatment of patients suffering from high blood pressure.

We were able to show Group management and the Board that we were on the right track. The expansion of our resources that the Board had approved with great reluctance in September 1964 had brought results.

The knowledge we gained during the alprenolol project made it possible for us to start and carry out the project that, in 1975, resulted in what became the Astra Group's most important product during the 80's. Metoprolol, was first approved for the treatment of high blood pressure and later for treating heart disease. It has been used by ten million patients and for several years reached annual sales of USD 400 million.

Our efforts to produce a medicine for the treatment of diseases of the heart and blood vessels had proved to be worthwhile, but the decisions had not been easy or obvious.

In the Fall of 1958, when we planned to build up resources for biological research, I tried to find an area where urgent medical needs, and our own potential, might coincide. I was looking for a field in which we could, in the long term, become specialists.

111

To gain some guidance, I interviewed a number of senior physicians at hospitals in Gothenburg, Lund and Stockholm.

There turned out to be as many needs as doctors to interview, but within most areas where they indicated urgent needs, it was difficult to find leads from which to start meaningful projects.

It was Lars Werkö who talked us into making heart and blood vessel illnesses a priority area. I had worked with Lars Werkö at the Pharmaceutical Society's research laboratory in Stockholm as early as 1947-1954. When he became Professor of Medicine at the University of Gothenburg, and Chief Physician at the University Hospital in 1957, we renewed our association.

Heart and blood vessel diseases were then, as now, the most common cause of death. Infectious diseases, which at one time caused the most fatalities, had successfully been fought with vaccines, penicillin and other antibiotics.

The basic research that had been carried out at Björn Folkow's department at the University was of great value in understanding the origins of high blood pressure and heart ailments.

The clinical research done at Lars Werkö's clinic gave us an opportunity to follow developments within cardiology, the study of the diseases and functioning of the heart. We could count on help in our discussions of goals and test results. This help in the testing and evaluating of the drugs we hoped to develop was an important reason for our choosing this field. Considering our limited resources, we could only work on one of the existing needs that had been outlined to us. Werkö advised us to try to develop a remedy for treating arrhythmias, or irregular heart beats. There were, at that time, virtually no medicines for patients suffering from these symptoms.

Quinidine from the Cinchona Tree

One of the few remedies physicians could give patients with arrhythmias were tablets containing quinidine extracted from the bark of the cinchona tree. These tablets had to be taken four times a day which could be annoying for patients who had to take them for several years. In addition, there were often side effects.

Werkö suggested that we should first test our time-release Durules.

The slow timed release of quinidine from Durules could be expected to reduce the risk of side effects. If the tablets only had to be administered mornings and evenings, this would be a significant improvement for the patients.

The company's marketing department was not enthusiastic about the project. The use of quinidine was so limited that it would hardly be worth spending several years working on such a project. Even if our projected preparation was better than the quinidine tablets already on the market, they didn't think sales would be enough to cover the development costs.

The medical need convinced us, however, to go ahead with the project. In 1958 John Sjögren was assigned to develop quinidine Durules.

After three years of work, the Quinidine Durules were ready to be tested at Lars Werkö's clinic. They proved to be a vast improvement over the other remedies being used at the clinic at that time. The clinical tests and evaluations of the remedy became part of a doctoral dissertation by one of the researchers at the clinic.

Sales of quinidine Durules were several times greater that what we had expected. The remedy became Hässle's first export product. For more than twenty-five years it has been used by tens of thousands of patients generating hundreds of thousands of dollars in annual sales.

Heart Fibrillations

The quinidine Durules were effective on patients with the kind of arrhythmias we call atrium fibrillations when the disorder is in the atriums or auricles of the heart. But the most serious form of ineffective cardiac rhythms involves compulsive contractions of the muscle fibres in the ventricles of the heart, ventricular fibrillations. There was nothing to indicate that quinidine would have an effect on this serious condition, which is one of the most common causes of sudden death.

When someone experiences ventricular fibrillations there is a sudden chaos in the precise electrical pulses in the venticulars of the heart. The normal impulses that control the regular beating of the heart muscle change to rapid signals that cause irregular contractions. This means that the heart muscle no longer can pump blood to the organs of the body.

113

Werkö underlined how important it was to find a medicine that would prevent this dangerous form of arrhythmia. An effective remedy would probably give many of these patients several more active years.

In our discussions on how a project should be started to find an arrhythmia drug that would prevent ventricular fibrillations, Björn Folkow said there were animal experiments which showed that these contractions could be triggered by the stress hormones adrenaline and noradrenaline. It was known that these hormones, which can cause palpitations of the heart, and sometimes irregular cardiac rhythms, are produced in increased amounts by physical or emotional stress.

The release of these stress hormones is determined by signals from the sympathetic nervous system. This system carries messages from the "stress center" in the brain to the heart, as well as to other organs. If we could find a drug that protected the heart from these "stress signals", we could hope for positive effects on other kinds of arrhythmia as well as on other heart diseases.

How Can the Heart Be Protected From Stress?

We thought Folkow's suggestion was very interesting. These discussions were in 1959. In the Spring of 1960, we decided to start what was called the "Arrhythmia Project". The minutes of one of our "consultation conferences" states that the goal of the project was:

"To develop a medicine that would protect an ailing heart from over-stimulation caused by physical or emotional stress."

Nevertheless, we had no idea from which chemical structure we could start to develop substances for testing. We also lacked any clear idea of the working mechanism of the medicine we wanted to create.

An American Gives Us Some Ideas

Our pharmacologist, Lars Garberg, reported that there didn't seem to be any logical methods we could use to test the kind of arrhythmia drug we were looking for. He had spent a long time looking through publications and talking with researchers. He concluded that the project we had just started was one of the most difficult we could have involved ourselves in, mostly because of the lack of animal testing methods that could be expected to correspond to the arrhythmias the physicians wished to treat in human patients.

Garberg proved to be right. It would be thirty years before our researchers found a drug that we thought was worth testing on patients with ventricular arrhythmias. That was when we started a new project in the 80's and new testing methods had been developed.

Even if the project we started in the Summer of 1960 didn't produce the arrhythmia drug we'd hoped for, it did result in other useful drugs for the treatment of heart diseases and high blood pressure.

With Astra's help, we made contact with the American pharmacologist J. Roberts, at Cornell University in New York. He had some ideas about new drugs to fight arrhythmias. He had also been working on a new method to test arrhythmia drugs.

We invited Roberts to Gothenburg to discuss a possible cooperation. In August 1960 Lars Garberg, Björn Folkow, Lars Werkö and I had intensive discussions with Roberts. Even though he didn't seem to have a clear understanding of the working mechanism he was looking for, we thought it would be worthwhile to test his ideas and testing methods.

When Hans Corrodi visited Hässle in February 1960, he was appointed project manager for the Arrhythmia Project. In August 1960 he moved to Sweden and began working at Hässle. He synthesized a number of substances following the chemical structures that Roberts drew up for us.

But in the Spring of 1961 we were forced to conclude that we hadn't found any interesting effects in the substances we had tested and that it was meaningless to continue. We no longer believed in the ideas of our American consultant. We looked for a new way forward.

The New Way

So in May 1961 I appealed to Arvid Carlsson for help. That was when he outlined the principle that is described in the chapter: "A New Road Towards the Goal".

For this project, he suggested that we should develop clinically useful beta-receptor blockers, or beta-blockers. This was the first time I had heard this idea with which I came to share my life over the next quarter century.

He advised our chemists to start their work with a compound called DCI, developed by the Lilly company in the United States.

Locks and Keys Control the Heart

The working mechanism of the kind of drug we decided to attempt to develop can best be described as locks and keys.

When a person is confronted with a stressful situation, the sympathetic nervous system is stimulated to release the signal substance noradrenalin directly to the heart. In addition, adrenaline is released from the adrenal glands, and reaching the heart through the blood. Noradrenalin and adrenaline enter through special receptors in the heart muscle cells.

These receptors are a kind of lock where adrenaline and noradrenalin enter as keys. When the lock is opened, the heart is stimulated to increased activity. It beats harder and faster.

Beta-blockers are like keys that fit into the locks, but can't open them. So they protect the heart from the stress caused by adrenaline and noradrenalin by stopping these hormones from entering the receptors. This has been shown to be of great importance to an ailing heart. Beta-blockers can save patients' lives and prevent sudden death after a heart attack.

In 1988, when Arvid Carlsson and I went over our notes and memories of the discussions we had when the project began, he told me:

"At a symposium in the United States in 1958 I heard the pharmacologist, James Slater talk about the compound DCI. Researchers at the American pharmaceutical company Lilly had synthesized a compound that seemed to represent a new pharmacological principle. They called it the adrenerg beta receptor blocker. Lilly's scientists hoped that DCI could be used to treat disturbances in the activity of the heart.

"According to what Slater later wrote in a journal, he had no clear idea of how DCI would affect a patient. In co-operation with a hospi-

116

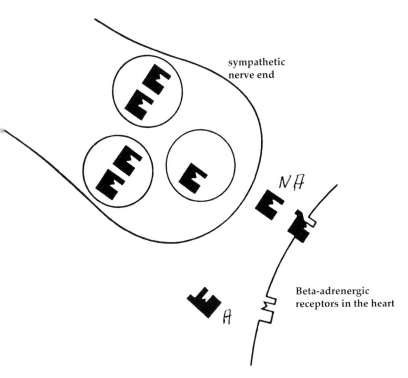

sympathetic
nerve end

Beta-adrenergic
receptors in the heart

Schematic picture of how beta-blockers work to protect the heart. The dark figure in
the receptor on the heart symbolizes a beta-blocker that sits in the way of the stress
hormones adrenaline (A) and noradrenaline (NA), which are unable to act on the receptor.

tal DCI was tested on three patients with severe heart disorders. All
available medicines had already been tried to no avail. As a last resort,
they tried DCI. But all three patients then showed overly-increased
heart activity, tachycardia, and one died. This was certainly because of
the severe heart disease, but Lilly's researchers couldn't ignore the
possibility that DCI could have had a negative effect on that sick heart.
They never dared test DCI again. They synthesized and tested more
than a hundred more compounds hoping for one that didn't cause tachycardia. When they didn't succeed, the project was discontinued.

Arvid sat quietly for a moment, recalling: "When I heard about

DCI's side effects, I remember thinking that DCI shouldn't be seen as the end result of an interesting principle. It should be seen as the beginning of a new method for treating heart ailments. Which disorders, I didn't know. That was why I advised Hässle to start the synthesis program with DCI. You would create variations and work towards a drug that didn't have DCI's side effects."

Arvid continued: "Shortly after we moved into our new premises here in May, 1960, we were visited by Dr. Neil Moran from Atlanta, Georgia. He was a guest researcher at the Karolinska Institute in Stockholm, and held a very interesting seminar for us on pharmacology.

"In 1957 Dr. Moran heard Slater report on DCI. He had asked for a sample of the compound. When he published his results, Moran used the term adrenerga beta-receptor blockers. This was probably the first time the new mechanism had received that name in a publication. In his lecture, Moran described these beta-blockers as interesting pharmacological tools."

Arvid explained how, within pharmacology at that time, interest was growing in the concept of receptors which I have tried to describe in terms of locks and keys. He explained how a modern pharamcologist thinks:

"What we are looking for are compounds that block the effects of the body's own signal substances on different receptors which are the cells' signal receivers. You can call these signal substances messengers. We gain deeper knowledge of how drugs work through such studies. This gives us better opportunities to create better medicines.

"Moran's lecture increased my interest in DCI, and in using beta-blockers as a tool. My main interest was the brain. Dr. Moran himself was most interested in the heart. It was after Moran's visit that we seriously began to discuss using beta-blockers in Hässle's research into medicines for the heart."

Arvid advised our project group to look beyond finding remedies for arrhythmias. Other heart illnesses might also react positively to these new drugs.

118

The Beta-Blocker Project

After the summer of 1961, we started working intensively on the project. The pharmacologists developed new test methods. The chemists had in DCI an interesting structure as their starting point. During the next few years, more than three hundred compounds were synthesized and tested.

Thanks to our test methods, the pharmacologists and chemists could draw useful conclusions from practically every compound that was tested. We hoped that the new drugs that could come out of the project would be important medicines for treating several different kinds of heart complaints.

Heart Diseases

When we started the beta-blocker project in 1961, it was totally unknown if this new principle would be of value in healthcare. We had many lively discussions about the risks of side effects. Warnings were expressed during our meetings with the clinics with which we were working. There were those who thought that these new compounds would just remain interesting tools in the pharmacologists' laboratories.

It was not easy to argue for the project with Group management and our marketing director. There was no market to study, of course, since we wouldn't even say which heart disorders we thought could be treated if we succeeded in producing clinically useful beta-blockers.

During discussions at consultation conferences and through contacts at seminars and conferences, we tried to learn more about the illnesses that might be treated with these drugs.

Angina Pectoris

Physicians usually tell patients that pain in their chests is caused by "vascular spasms in the heart".

For the heart muscle to be able to do its work and pump blood to all the organs of the body, it needs oxygen and nourishment every second. These are provided to the cells of heart from the blood through the coronary arteries which run along the outside the heart.

When the heart is subjected to major strain because of physical or mental exertions, it needs more oxygen quickly. A healthy heart matches the supply of blood to its oxygen requirements. If the coronary arteries are constricted by arteriosclerosis, the blood can't get through and there's an oxygen shortage. The heart sends out signals in the form of pain. The patient then gets attacks of vascular spasms, making it impossible to walk. He has to rest, and should take a medicine to help the heart get more oxygen.

When we started this research project, the only remedies available to us were various nitroglycerin preparations. These expand the coronary arteries so that the blood can get through. Then the pain ceases.

We thought that there ought to be another way of preventing these attacks of angina pectoris. One way would be to protect the heart from stress so that it didn't need as much oxygen. We hoped that our beta-blockers would have that effect by inhibiting the stress hormones which want to press the heart to work harder than it can handle.

During the mid-60's our reasoning was confirmed several times. Clinical tests carried out in Britain showed promising results with the first beta-blocker that was clinically used. This was a drug from the British company ICI. Their research group and ours had independently found clinically useful beta-blockers. Our own studies also showed that our beta-blocker was very effective against angina pectoris. Beta-blockers are now part of the basic therapy for this disease.

Arteriosclerosis

Beta-blockers had a demonstrably positive effect on the symptoms of angina pectoris, but we also asked ourselves if the beta-blockers could affect the disease that lay behind the symptoms, arteriosclerosis, the hardening or clogging of the heart's coronary arteries? Such an effect would mean that these medicines didn't just free patients from pain after exertion, improving the quality of their lives, but would also increase their chances of living longer.

Hardening of the arteries, arteriosclerosis, is the commonest cause of angina pectoris and heart attacks as well as thrombosis in the brain. The inner walls of the arteries thicken because of deposits of fat as well as calcium. This process goes on all our lives, but becomes a problem when we reach middle age. For some people, the wall-thickening process by then has reduced the inner diameter of the arteries so much that the flow of blood to the heart is impeded. This can lead to angina pectoris.

Arteriosclerosis also increases the risk of blood clots clogging the arteries, completely cutting off blood to the heart which can cause a heart attack. If the blood is prevented from reaching the brain, a stroke can result.

Why are so many people affected by arteriosclerosis? The reasons are not completely clear. As early as thirty years ago the importance of a proper diet and a healthy lifestyle were being discussed. There were also studies that indicated that mental stress increased the risk of complications arising from arteriosclerosis. We saw a possibility that beta-blockers would be able to protect the heart so that the risk of heart attacks and sudden death could be reduced.

These discussions during our consultant conferences motivated us to support the comprehensive survival studies that were carried out with our beta-blockers during the period 1969–1988. These included studies of patients who had suffered heart attacks.

Heart Attacks (Myocardial Infarction)

When the coronary vessels that supply the heart with blood are clogged so that part of the heart muscle doesn't receive enough oxygen, severe pain arises. This painful seizure in the chest can come suddenly and without warning. A patient who has had chest pains from physical and mental stress for a long time, can have had these pains because of angina pectoris. But the pains of a heart attack are longer-lasting. Patients who suffer long and severe chest pains should be taken immediately to the hospital. Half a million people die every year in the United States because of heart attacks.

The supply of blood to part of the heart is most often impeded during a heart attack by a blood clot. When that part of the heart muscle receives too little oxygen, there's a risk that it will be so severely injured that the muscle cells die.

From the early 60's several Swedish hospitals opened special wards where patients who had suffered severe heart attacks could be intensively observed and monitored. This improved their chances of survival. Life-threatening arrhythmias were treated with electric shocks which normalized the rhythm of the heart.

Heart Arrhythmias

Before the 60's there were no drugs which could prevent or treat ventricular arrhythmias.

Around 1960, an American cardiologist discovered that Astra's local anaesthetic, lidocain could normalize some life-threatening heart arrhythmias. When President Eisenhower was treated with lidocain for a serious arrhythmia, the drug became widely known.

There was evidence from several parts in the world that intensive care improved a patient's chances of survival following a heart attack. But there were no drugs that could help patients avoid further attacks from occurring. Here was an urgent need. There was a possibility that the protective effect of the beta-blockers on the heart could reduce the risk of new attacks. Perhaps these drugs could prevent an attack in a small part of the heart from spreading to other parts. Could these drugs prevent sudden death?

We knew nothing about this when we discussed the potential importance of these new heart medicines in the early 60's. Thanks to our close contact with Björn Folkow and his colleagues at the University's Department of Physiology, and the cardiologists who were trained at Lars Werkö's clinic, we had an insight into these questions at an early stage. We were also given suggestions for carrying out tests which were to be of great importance in getting international attention for our beta-blockers.

Hypertonia – High Blood Pressure

As a rule, a moderate increase in blood pressure doesn't cause any discomfort, but in the long term, high blood pressure means an increased risk of a heart attack or stroke occurring. This is why it's important that high blood pressure be treated. Since patients seldom feel discomfort from such high blood pressure, it can be difficult for a doctor to motivate them to take a medicine daily to lower their blood pressure to a more desirable level. This is why it's essential that medicines to reduce blood pressure can be taken without unpleasant side effects.

Use of the first medicines to reduce blood pressure began during the 50's. They caused such severe side effects that patients refused to take them.

During the late 50's and early 60's diuretics began to be used. These drugs were a great step forward. They reduce blood pressure by eliminating water and salts from the blood. With them, for the first time, doctors had access to medicines that patients could be induced to take for long periods without much discomfort.

There are several factors which act together to regulate blood pressure. For that reason, physicians need access to drugs with different working mechanisms in order to treat their patients. In difficult cases it can be necessary to use several drugs together.

When we discussed the need for better drugs to treat high blood pressure at consultation conferences between 1960 and 1975, Björn Folkow always underlined how important it would be to produce a medicine that dilated the small arterial blood vessels. By dilating these, blood pressure could be reduced and the heart would no longer need to work as hard to pump blood through the narrow vessels.

Because of the research carried out at Björn Folkow's department, we knew that muscle fibres in the walls of the blood vessels get stronger and the blood vessel walls thicker the more the blood vessels are exposed to high blood pressure. The effect is the same as when the biceps of the upper arm is exercised by pull-ups. The muscle gets stronger and bigger. When the walls of the blood vessels thicken, the channel through the blood vessel grows narrower. That means that it's more difficult for the blood to flow through the vessel. The blood pressure rises, which further contributes to the thickening of the blood vessel walls. We hoped that blood pressure reducing medicines would reverse this process. Tests on rats with hereditary high blood pressure demonstrated that these theories were correct.

The chapter: "The University Doors Opened" describes how these discussions with Björn Folkow led to a new project being started in 1975. After thirteen years of work, the drug felodipin was registered. It has been described as the most effective medicine in existence for reducing blood pressure.

During the early 60's we had many discussions about possible ways of treating heart diseases with beta-blockers. But none of us thought that such a drug could also be used to treat high blood pressure. According to the minutes from a meeting in 1961, Lars Werkö pointed out that beta-blockers could probably lower blood pressure. This was actually a warning at that time, since it might have been a problem when treating heart arrhythmias and angina pectoris. Now that we know that the most important use for beta-blockers is to lower blood pressure to treat hypertonia, it's interesting to recall this discussion where we only saw the lowering of blood pressure as a risk.

As early as 1963-65, Lars Werkö was telling us, however, that the results of his own and others' studies indicated that beta-blockers could have a good effect on patients whose blood pressure was too high. But despite beta-blockers having been used for more than twenty years to treat high blood pressure, the mechanism behind their effect is still not completely understood.

We know that the effect seen after a patient takes a beta-blocker is mainly due to a smoother heart function. Less blood is pumped every second and blood pressure drops. For long term treatment, other effects are more important. The thickening of the walls of the blood vessels is reversed and the blood pressure continues to decrease.

Undesirable Effects

The possible risks of side effects from the new medicines were discussed at the consultation conferences we held twice a year.

For the heart to be able to adjust the supply of blood to the requirements of the various organs of the body, the heart needs to be stimulated by the sympathetic nervous system. The blockers remove this stimulating effect. This might impair heart function, especially among patients suffering from vascular spasms and arrhythmias.

To reduce this risk, we set a goal of producing a drug with a weak stimulating effect. Our medicine wouldn't just sit in the lock and prevent adrenaline and noradrenaline from acting on the heart in stressful situations. It would have some capacity to open the lock so that the heart at rest receive the stimulation it is accustomed to.

There are beta receptors in the trachea, the windpipes. Their job is to enlarge the trachea so that more oxygen can enter the lungs. When you give a patient a beta-blocker to protect the heart or lower the blood pressure, there is a risk that these drugs will make it more difficult for asthma patients to get air into their lungs. We suspected that this might be a side effect of the medicine we wanted to produce. To reduce this risk, we decided in 1964 that the substance we developed should also have a stimulating effect on the trachea. This was the same idea that lay behind our ambition to ensure that the heart received stimulation as well.

The result of these discussions was the drug alprenolol, which was ready for use in the Fall of 1967.

What Have Others Done?

When researchers at a pharmaceutical company succeed in creating useful medicines, it's natural that physicians and patients are impressed by their accomplishment. It's easy to forget the important contributions made by university researchers over the years. Without the knowledge gained by basic research, no meaningful projects could be started.

One of the prerequisites for carrying out goal-oriented projects aimed at producing beta-blockers was knowledge of the stress hormones adrenaline and noradrenaline. When I investigated where our understanding of these hormones came from, I found interesting examples of how researchers had worked hard for many years in the pursuit of knowledge.

The most interesting thing was to see how discoveries in one country stimulate researchers in other parts of the world to new revelations that complement the earlier work. As far as adrenaline and noradrenaline were concerned, the understanding we had in 1960 was the result of important work in Britain, the United States, Japan, Germany, Austria and Sweden.

As always with pioneering new contributions to research, you never know when or where they will come. That's why it is so difficult to guide basic research.

During the 19th Century and towards its end it was believed that some form of electric impulses carried the signals from nerves to the heart. But had the signals to the heart actually worked this way, we would never have been able to develop "stress-protecting" beta-blockers.

Through a series of discoveries, researchers in different countries found explanations for the mechanisms that control the heart's activities. The first discovery was made in 1895. More than fifty years later, in 1948, the theories that provided the foundation for our research were published.

It was certainly a strange experiment that the English doctor, George Oliver, carried out on his own son in 1894. He had made an extract from the adrenal glands of calves which he injected into his son's foot. From today's point of view regarding safety and human trials, Oliver's experiment was completely unacceptable.

Oliver saw that the blood vessels in the foot contracted. He realized that he had made an interesting discovery, of which he was unable to interpret the significance. He did succeed in talking his friend, E.A. Schaffer, Professor of Physiology at the University of London, into studying the effects of the extract on dogs. Schaffer found that it greatly increased blood pressure.

Oliver and Schaffer published their observations in 1895.

The American biochemist John Abel tried to isolate the active substance in the adrenal gland and determine its chemical structure. He almost accomplished his goal, but didn't succeed completely. A Japanese biochemist named Jokiski Takamine, who was visiting Abel's laboratory in Washington, followed the experiment with interest. At home in Japan, he continued from where Abel had left off and succeeded, in 1901, in producing a pure crystallized substance which he called adrenaline. The stress hormone had been discovered.

Several years after this discovery, Takamine travelled back to Washington where he planted a Japanese cherry tree outside Abel's laboratory in gratitude for the idea he had been given there.

Independent of Takamine, the American Paul Aldrich isolated the same substance and determined the chemical structure of adrenaline.

The German chemist, Frederich Stolz produced adrenaline synthetically in 1904. He also synthesized a closely related compound, which he called noradrenaline, which means adrenaline without a certain group of atoms attached to a nitrogen atom. However, he didn't know that noradrenaline was of biological interest. That discovery took another forty years to make.

Despite our knowing, since 1895, that an extract of the adrenal gland had an effect on the blood vessels, and that the chemical structure of adrenaline since 1901, most researchers clung to the theory of electrical pulses from the nerves to the muscles. This shows how difficult it is for new ways of thinking and new ideas to gain acceptance.

A number of scientists, however, began to doubt the electrical signal theory. One of the most prominent was the British physiologist, T.R. Elliott. In 1905 he published an article in which he claimed that the transfer of signals from the nerves to the organs follows chemical paths with the release of adrenaline.

The Austrian pharmacologist, Otto Loewi, succeeded in a brilliant experiment in demonstrating that it is chemical substances that carry the signals. He published the results of his work in 1921 and was rewarded with the Nobel Prize for his discovery.

It is said that Loewi had long thought about how he should conduct the experiment. How could he prove that it was chemical substances, rather than electrical signals, that transferred the impulses to the heart?

One night he woke up after dreaming how the experiment should be carried out. In the morning, he was unable to read the notes he'd hurriedly made in the middle of the night, but after a moment's reflection, he remembered the experiment he'd dreamed of.

Noradrenaline was long regarded as a chemical curiosity until the Swedish physiologist, Ulf von Euler published in 1946 the results of experiments that demonstrated that noradrenaline is released as a signal substance in the nerve ends of the sympathetic nervous system. Twenty years later, he received the Nobel Prize in recognition of the discovery.

In 1948, the Swedish-American pharmacologist, R.P. Ahlquist published observations that became the foundation for the research that led to the creation of beta-blockers. He showed that the receptors which receive the signals from adrenaline and noradrenalin are of two types. He called them alpha receptors and beta receptors.

It was ten years before Ahlquist's theories of two different receptors, in what is called the adrenergic nervous system, was accepted by physiologists and pharamacologists. The final proof came in 1957 when C.E. Powell and J.H. Slater at the American pharmaceutical company, Eli Lilly, showed that the compound DCI could block the receptors which Ahlquist had called beta receptors, but didn't block the alpha receptors.

As mentioned previously, Lilly's researchers hoped that DCI would lead to a new type of medicine. When Slater reported on the unsuccessful patient trials carried out in 1958 Arvid Carlsson heard about the new principle of adrenergic beta receptor blockers. As related above, he passed that information on to us in 1961.

DCI also gave the British pharmacologist James Black the idea of developing drugs to combat heart disease. His goal was to find a medicine for angina pectoris and his work for the British pharmaceutical company ICI led to the first clinically usable beta-blocker, Inderal® (propranolol).

Independent of Black's ideas, and without knowing about the work at ICI, we started our own beta-blocker project. This is the research that led to the two drugs alprenolol and metoprolol.

It's interesting that only ICI in Britain and Hässle in Sweden succeeded in developing these successful drugs on the basis of what was known in the late 50's. At least five companies were trying to develop beta-blockers around 1960.

The American company, Eli Lilly made a pioneer contribution by developing the first beta-blocker, but when they didn't succeed in eliminating the side effects of DCI, they gave up. Another American company, Mead Johnsson, started about the same time as Lilly. Their beta-blocker, MJ1999, was developed as early as 1960, but it was never a success. Also in 1960, the German company, Boerhringer Ingelheim produced the beta-blocker, Kö446, but it was never developed into a medicine.

The reasons that only ICI and Hässle were successful in this area, and created both the first and second generation beta-blockers, are worth looking at. When Lennart Sölvell and I visited ICI's research center in England in May 1962, we didn't know about their work in this field. They had 735 researchers and technicians at Alderly Park. In comparison with Hässle's little group of 35 people, it's remarkable that we succeeded in the race.

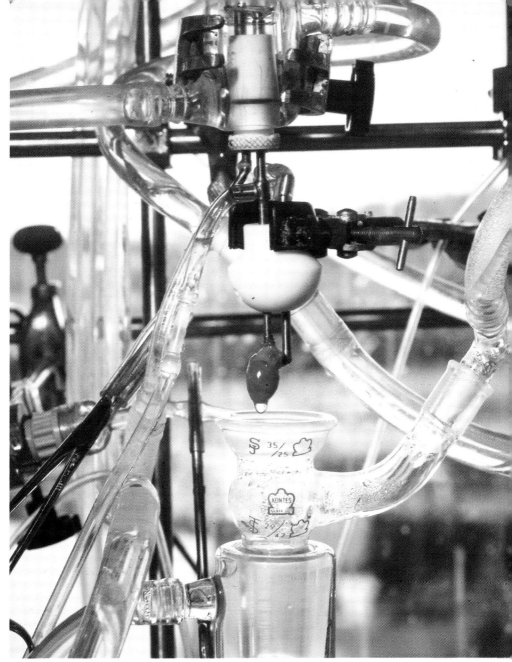

The picture shows a rat's heart studied for biochemical effects in the beta-blocker project.. *Hässle's archives.*

The First Set Back

The project got underway with great enthusiasm in 1961 and 1962. When the first compound, H29/50, was picked out for testing on healthy humans, we hoped it would meet our expectations. But on the first trials the physician found that the compound caused heart palpitations, tachycardia. This indicated that the compound had too much of a stimulating effect on the heart.

We rejected H29/50 and looked for a new compound with better characteristics. Our greatest problem was that practically every compound was blocked by other companies' patents. Most of them belonged to ICI, but Boehringer Ingelheim also had patents that hindered us.

Not only were all the compounds we synthesized covered by our competitors' patents, most of our ideas for new syntheses were blocked by new patents applications. During 1963 and 1964 we were close to discontinuing the project several times.

During the Spring of 1964 our chemists saw no way of getting through the patent obstacles. Even the otherwise always optimistic Arne Brändström said:

"It looks impossible. We can't get beyond our competitors' patents."

But, when we went though all the ideas and all the imaginable syntheses, it turned out that in our animal experiments two compounds, H56/28 and H49/43, had demonstrated the characteristics we were looking for. These compounds both had what is called an unsaturated side chain. Looking through the patents, we couldn't find any such compounds described. Arne Brändström had developed special methods for adding unsaturated side chains to molecular structures. We applied for patents applications to protect these two compounds.

New Possibilities

An event which turned out to have decisive importance was when pharmacologist, Bengt Åblad took over full responsibility for the project in March 1963.

130

In his doctoral dissertation, he had studied the effect of heart and blood pressure medicines. He had analyzed the results of animal experiments and compared them with the effects on patients and healthy test subjects. This information was of great value for our project.

The first really meaningful project plan was included in a memo from Bengt Åblad dated April 23, 1963. He outlined how drugs for both heart arrhythmias and angina pectoris should be tested and selected.

Bengt Åblad introduced new methods for animal experiments which provided us with more guidance for choosing the substances that could be expected to be clinically useful.

When Peder Berntsson, head of Hässle's Chemical Department between 1970 and 1988, and I discussed the reasons for our little group's success in developing useful medicines based on the beta-blocker principle where companies with much larger resources had failed with his comment was:

"Bengt Åblad was, along with James Black at ICI, probably the only researcher in the pharmaceutical industry in the 60's who understood what beta-blockers could do clinically. That gave us an advantage over our competitors. Another reason was that our pharmacologists and chemists worked together so constructively. Their co-operation was based on an interest in creating something and which wasn't prevented by formal meetings. During the years we worked with Ciba-Geigy, we learned how researchers at a Swiss company are bound by strict rules and formal decisions. At Hässle we had a kind of freedom."

Important Decisions

It was obvious that our limited resources were insufficient to bring both H56/28 and H49/43 to clinical trials. We had to decide at an early stage which to go on with. One decisive question was if the compounds could be absorbed in the intestinal canal, allowing them to be administered to patients in tablet form.

While the company was closed between Christmas and New Year in 1964, Bengt Åblad and his closest colleague tested both beta-blockers on themselves. During the previous Fall, we had carried out

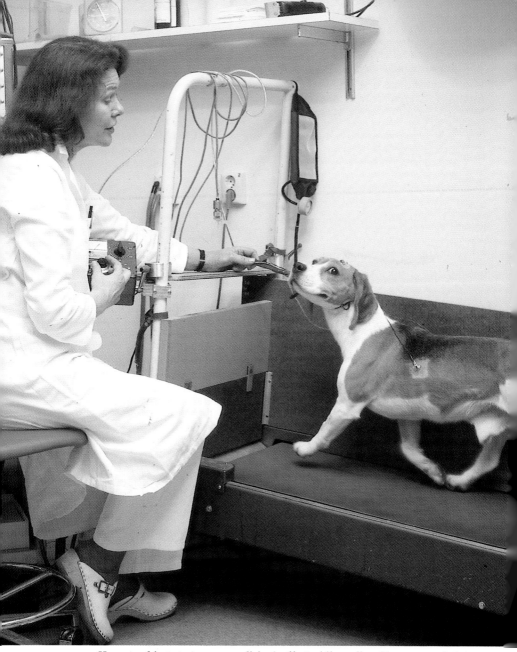

Human subjects test a new medicine's effect while cycling. Dogs are made to run on a treadmill. If the dog seems to be happily wagging its tail, that is seen as a sign that the new substance has no side effects. *Hässle's archives.*

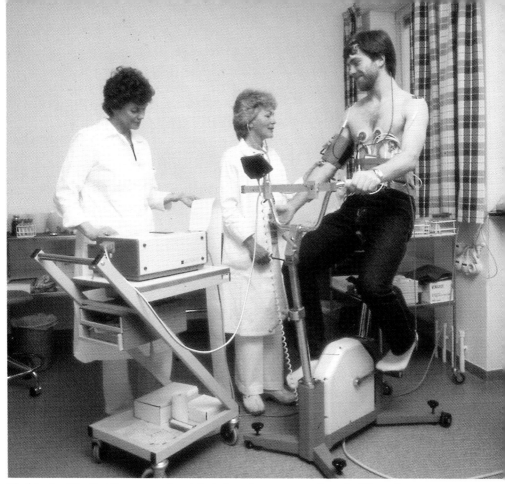

The big step: The first time a new drug is tested on a human, as a rule on healthy male subjects. After safety trials on various kinds of animals, a substance is first tested in very low doses, then in the doses that are hoped to have an effect on patients. *Hässle's archives.*

the safety trials that were required before they could be tested on humans, so they knew that the substances weren't dangerous. What Bengt Åblad did was compare the effect on himself after an injection with the effect from a capsule he swallowed. The injections of the test substances were administered by Lennart Sölvell at the Gothenburg University Hospital.

The first working day after the New Year's holiday I was told that we should concentrate on H56/28, which had demonstrated good absorption. The other substance had hardly been absorbed at all in the intestinal canal and was discarded from further consideration.

In consultation with Begnt Åblad, Lennart Sölvell carried out the first H56/28 studies on healthy subjects in the Spring of 1965. One of the most important milestones in the history of the company was the telephone call from Lennart Sölvell with the good news:

"It looks good. H56/28 has the beta-blocking effect we've been looking for. We haven't seen any side effects in the doses we've tested."

Success and Priorities

On the last day of the Astra Group's annual research conference in September, 1965 Begnt Oom, who was chairing the meeting, asked:

"Is there any of the Group's projects that ought to be given priority?"

Aldo Truant, Director of Research at Astra's laboratories in Worcester, Massachusetts, made an important contribution with his enthusiastic response:

"We have many projects at Astra, perhaps too many. But the project developing adrenergic beta-blockers with Hässle's H56/28 looks like the only project where we are breaking new ground. The British company, ICI is ahead of us with a substance with the same working mechanism. We don't yet know if doctors accept the new medicines, but the principle is promising. If Astra becomes the second company in the world to market a drug using a new principle, that's important in itself. Besides, H56/28 is different enough from ICI's Inderal to make it an interesting alternative for doctors."

Aldo Truant continued:

"If Astra has a chance to become a good number two ahead of all oher competitors who are just now beginning their research in this new area, we should make it a priority project and devote more resources to it than Hässle can manage by itself. Mr. Chairman, let's vote on it. Everyone who votes to give H56/28 the highest priority among the Group's projects should also be prepared to help and support the project."

The chairman accepted the proposal. Research directors and medical advisors at the research and development organizations in our three centres in Sweden as well as in the United States took part in the vote. The recommendation was that H56/28 be given the highest priority.

For various reasons, it was only Aldo Truant who took it upon himself to carry out studies with H56/28, but he had no opportunity for any direct participation in the project. The other research directors felt so bound by their own projects that they were unable to contribute to the work on H56/28 so we at Hässle had to do everything, but with no increase in our budget. Despite the recommendation that H56/28 be given the Group's highest priority, this was not reflected in our budget during the following two years. The only explanation I have for this is that the marketing people and economists were pessimistic about our ability to succeed in this new area. It was too new. There was no market for them to analyze.

But giving the priority to the project made a big difference internally at Hässle. Everyone felt strongly motivated to do everything to develop H56/28 into a medicine as quickly as possible. It was easier to reapportion resources within our own organization to the priority project, but we really needed the greater resources that we hoped the priority designation would lead to.

After the research conference in September, 1965 we agreed at Hässle on a plan to have H56/28 ready for registration in the Fall of 1966 with the aim of having it on the market by the Fall of 1967. It was an optimistic and daring plan. The various safety trials had already begun. That meant that H56/28 would be tested on rats and dogs over a long period of time. The doses would have to be much higher than those which would be used for the clinical trials. A number of other safety tests would also be carried out, including cancer tests and a study of the risk of birth defects.

Together with technicians at Astra's factory in Södertälje, we worked out a method to produce H56/28 and to make tablets.

In order to get permission from the ethical committees and the Social Welfare Board to start clinical trials, reports had to be submitted with the results of all of these studies.

The Project is in Danger

On November 17, 1965 we invited the three physicians who had taken part in the first clinical studies to a conference to discuss their results. We looked forward to the meeting with great excitement and were hoping to get the go-ahead for expanded clinical tests.

The three Swedish physicians were sceptical to say the least. When the first results were less positive than had been hoped for, the tests had been called off. No disturbing side effects had been noted, but the effect on angina pectoris was not as promising as we had hoped.

During later tests it turned out that the dose we had recommended had been too low.

What was most disturbing was that no positive effects on arrhythmia patients had been found. The opinion of the clinicians was that it wasn't worth continuing to test H56/28.

Fortunately, a group of doctors at a hospital in Tampere, Finland had also tested H56/28 for a number of months. When the first results on patients with heart arrhythmia there were positive, the medical director at the clinic, Eino Linko, had encouraged his colleagues to increase the number of patients. He could demonstrate positive effects on all 43 patients who received the drug, citing their electrocardiograms.

The Swedish and Finnish doctors had chosen different kinds of arrhythmias for their tests. The new drug apparently only affected the type of patients that had been chosen in Finland.

If H56/28 had not been tested in Finland at an early stage, and had not shown positive results there, the project probably would have been discontinued. If we hadn't succeeded in getting our chosen substance to registration and marketing in the Fall of 1967, it would have taken too long to develop an alternative. By that time, many other pharmaceutical companies around the world would have gotten into the race for better beta-blockers. We would have had a hard time fighting against that kind of competition.

Comprehensive Clinical Trials

In the Fall of 1965, we hired a young physician to lead and co-ordinate the clinical tests that were to be carried out in a number of countries.

136

Gunnar Nyberg was a local physician who had contacted Hässle looking for more stimulating and challenging work. While working with the documentation of H56/28, he specialized in studies of angina pectoris. His doctoral dissertation dealt with clinical methods for evaluating medicines for this illness.

The double-blind clinical tests that Per Björntorp carried out at Gothenburg's University Hospital, where he later became professor and Chief Physician, were of decisive importance for demonstrating the value of H56/28 for angina pectoris. The 13 patients who went through the tests and experienced beneficial effects from the treatment for many years, were followed very carefully during this entire period.

Eino Linko's results on arrhythmia patients became the most important proof of the effect of H56/28 on that illness.

When these tests in the Nordic countries convinced us that H56/28 was a useful medicine, we planned and carried out clinical trials in many other countries. In Britain, we hired physician Brian Commerford, who worked part-time at a hospital in London where he carried out several studies at the same time helping us make other contacts in Britain.

Some of the best planned studies were carried out in Australia, where Professor John Hickie co-ordinated the tests at a number of heart clinics.

Unfortunately, we never succeeded in starting any clinical trials in the United States. So our first original medicine was never introduced on to the large American market.

Mysterious Deaths

A telex message from Helsinki in 1966 scared us deeply:

"Two patients have died during the clinical trials of H56/28. All tests in Finland have been stopped."

When Gunnar Nyberg arrived at the Meiland Clinic in Helsinki the following day, the atmosphere was tense. But when the code on the tablet packages was deciphered, it turned out that neither of the two patients who had died had received H56/28. They belonged to the group that received placebo tablets.

The patients in this clinical trial had angina pectoris. All of them received the usual medical treatment for this complaint. To test the new drug, the patients also received a tablet with a code number. Half of the number of patients received H56/28 and half received placebo tablets. The tests were double-blind, as neither the doctors nor the patients knew which tablets contained the active drug.

The patients had died because of the seriousness of their heart disease, but had they been in the group receiving H56/28, the new drug probably would have been blamed. We would have been in the same situation as the American company, Lilly when they discarded DCI after a death. It is very difficult to determine cause and effect. There are certainly many pitfalls in a research project's long journey from idea to finished medicine.

Two years later we received a similarly alarming telex from Astra's office in Sydney, Australia. Two patients had died at a hospital in Hobarth, in Tasmania. They were taking part in one of ten studies being led by Professor Hickie. The trials were skilfully set-up and until then had gone well. Now all tests in Australia had been suspended.

Gunnar Nyberg immediately flew to Australia. He and the Medical Director at Astra's Sydney office flew on to Tasmania.

At the hospital, the staff was upset and indignant. The doctors were convinced that the new drug had caused the deaths, but once again it turned out that neither of the two patients had received H56/28.

We were greatly relieved, since this meant our drug had still not shown any risk to health, and the clinical tests in Australia could continue. After a couple of years, Professor Hickie and the other participating doctors published their results. These were very positive and supported our belief that H56/28 would be useful for the treatment of angina pectoris.

None of the patients who received H56/28 had died, but several in the placebo groups had. It was quite possible that the drug had actually saved the lives of some of the patients who might have otherwise died, but the studies hadn't proved this and we were careful to avoid making such a claim at that time.

Improved Survival

A few years later, studies were carried out which confirmed that beta-blockers, such as H56/28, which by then had received the name alprenolol, did in fact reduce the risk of sudden death after a heart attack. These medicines did save lives.

The study that first demonstrated this using alprenolol was carried out in Gothenburg. The results were published in the British medical journal, "The Lancet" in November, 1974 by Anders Vedin, Claes Wilhelmsson, Lars Willhelmsen, Gösta Tiblin and Lars Werkö. In the study, a number of patients who had suffered heart attacks were followed for two years. Some were given alprenolol, the others a placebo. The survival rate was significantly higher among the group treated with alprenolol.

A False Alarm from Poland

Alprenolol was marketed in many countries under the name of Aptin, but it was never sold in Poland because a Polish professor became convinced that it caused damage to the liver, despite questionable evidence to support his belief.

A short time after Gunnar Nyberg had interested a doctor in Poland in carrying out clinical trials of H56/28, we received a telex from our representative in that country. The professor who was to study the safety of the drug before it could be administered to patients had observed liver damage in healthy test subjects so the planned tests of patients could not begin.

Because of our animal tests and studies of healthy test subjects, we were sure that H56/28 did not affect the liver, but the Polish professor was convinced that the drug was harmful. He had used a different method for his tests. To make sure, we repeated the tests using the same method that had been used in Poland. But we still couldn't find any indication of liver damage.

It is likely that the students he used for his tests had been drinking alcohol the night before the trials were carried out. That would have caused the results he found in the liver tests.

Television

While on a visit to Stockholm in early 1967, Arvid Carlsson and I ran into Swedish Television's science reporter, Bengt Feldreich and the secretary of the National Medical Research Council.

The Council's annual report that year had mentioned that an interesting joint research project was underway between the Faculty of Medicine at the University of Gothenburg and the pharmaceutical company Hässle. Bengt Feldreich, who had for several years successfully presented the frontlines of research for TV viewers, expressed interest and discussed a report on our project with Arvid Carlsson.

A few months later a TV team arrived in Gothenburg and made a program called "Medicine for the Millions". It followed the process from basic research at the university to the testing of the new drug on healthy subjects and finally on patients. That was as far as the project had gotten at that point. We didn't know for sure if and when H56/28 would be accepted by the authorities.

The last question that I was asked during our interview was: "Can it be right for a private company to take advantage of state financed basic research carried out at the University of Gothenburg and earn money from the resulting drug?"

My answer was: "If we at Hässle, after seven years work and a million dollars in project costs, develop a useful medicine, then it is first of all the patients who will profit from it. We hope the country will gain from the export income. That we get money to finance new research projects is, I think, something that everyone profits from."

Aptin a Useful Medicine

At the end of October, 1967 H56/28, alprenolol, was registered in Sweden under the name of Aptin. At about the same time, it was approved in West Germany and during the following months approval came in a number of other countries.

Our goal for the project when it started had been to develop a drug for the treatment of heart arrhythmia. Aptin was approved for the treatment of a particular kind of arrhythmia. The documentation we presented demonstrated the drug's value, especially for the treatment of angina pectoris.

140

"The Alprenolol Team" in 1963. From the left: Hans Corrodi, project manager 1960-62; Bengt Åblad, project manager 1963-67; Arne Brändström, Director of Chemical Research; behind him can be seen a glimpse of Lars Ek, Bengt Åblad's colleague; Ivan Östholm, chairman and Research Director; with his back to the camera, Lars Garberg, Director of the Pharmacology Laboratory; Lennart Sölvell, medical consultant and advisor can be glimpsed behind Margit Brogård, pharmacologist; at the far right, scientific advisor, Arvid Carlsson.

It was at the end of 1969 when we first received results from the clinical trials that showed that Aptin lowered blood pressure in patients suffering from hypertonia. This indication was later approved by the authorities in a number of countries.

After extensive clinical tests, we could document that Aptin reduced the risk of sudden death in patients who had suffered heart attacks.

When the documentation was available for all the indications, it was clear that Aptin was a useful medicine. Nevertheless, it took a

141

long time to convince doctors of the value of beta-blockers. In several countries, physicians were negative to the idea. It was several years before this form of treatment was finally accepted in virtually all countries.

Particularly in West Germany, doctors feared that these drugs could have an injurious effect on the heart. Alprenolol, which was also sold under the name of Aptin in West Germany, was for several years a very minor product in that country. However, it turned out that sales per inhabitant in one district were several times higher than in other parts of West Germany. One of the medical representatiors, Andreas Feulner, had succeeded in understanding the documentation and the medical value of the drug better than his colleagues in other districts. Because of this he succeeded in convincing doctors that they should use the drug.

When Andreas Feulner, a few years later became the president of Astra's subsidiary in West Germany, he succeeded in making the company one of the most successful pharmaceutical companies in the country and Astra's largest foreign subsidiary.

No Marketing in the United States

An innovation becomes important when the product that results reaches or exceeds the expectations of its innovators. Alprenolol was the largest selling drug in Sweden for several years, but abroad it was never the big-seller we had hoped for. Even if sales were between USD 15 and 20 million a year for several years, our expectations had been much higher. Astra's foreign subsidiaries and agents had marketed the local anaesthetic, lidocain with great success for many years, but these organizations lacked the competence and resources to introduce a medicine for the treatment of heart diseases. It would be several years before we would develop that ability.

When the marketing people in different countries encountered the initial scepticism among doctors for such a new medicine based on a completely new principle, they were naturally reluctant to invest their limited time and resources in a major campaign.

Our biggest disappointment was that alprenolol was never introduced in the United States. It was there that we had hoped for the large profits that would make it possible to carry out new projects with considerably better resources.

The management of Astra's American subsidiary maintained that cardiologists in the United States were so negative about beta-blockers that it would be difficult to market alprenolol.

On a visit to the U.S., I tried to convince Astra's local president, Mats Nilsson to start the clinical trials that would make possible the introduction of alprenolol. He told me that, several weeks before my visit, he had had a conversation with the chairman of Astra's board, Jacob Wallenberg. While visiting the United States, the chairman had asked Mats Nilsson why he wasn't marketing alprenolol in the United States. Jacob Wallenberg had referred him to Lars Werkö who was convinced that alprenolol was a valuable drug that ought to be marketed there.

But Mats Nilsson had told the chairman that the negative attitude towards this kind of drug among American cardiologists made this impossible.

During an interview in December, 1983 with Wallenberg's successor as chairman of the Astra board, Sten Gustafsson, I took up the question of why alprenolol had never been marketed in the United States. He agreed that the American doctors' apprehensions about beta-blockers would have made it difficult for Astra to introduce alprenolol, but it was not unlikely that the negative experience with the iron supplement Sorbifer might have contributed as well. Mats Nilsson had become sceptical of Hässle's products. He suspected that the quality and documentation did not live up to what was required by the authorities in the United States.

Since Astra's own subsidiary wasn't interested in alprenolol, the medicine was licensed to the American company, Warner Lambert. From a legal point of view the contract was skilfully drawn up. Had there ever been any sales of alprenolol in the United States, the Group would have earned good profits, but there was no chance that alprenolol would be registered and approved for sales.

According to the agreement, Hässle had to answer for practically all the documentation that was needed in the United States, but at that point, we lacked the resources to meet the commitments we already had in Europe and Australia. Gunnar Nyberg was the only physician at Hässle monitoring the clinical trials of alprenolol. He already had far too much to do. Despite this, he tried to help Warner Lambert get started, but as that company didn't have anybody with the necessary competence, there was nothing that could be done.

Then a new problem appeared in our co-operation with Warner Lambert. According to American anti-trust laws, you can't include a clause in a contract preventing a licensee from working with the products of a competing product. You have to trust that the licensee will wholeheartedly support the licensed product. In our contacts with American physicians, we discovered that the company had developed its own beta-blocker and was just starting clinical trials. This meant a conflict between their product and the one they had licensed from us. But despite spending a lot of money on developing and testing its own beta-blocker, Warner Lambert never succeeded in getting it approved for marketing.

A few years later, when we negotiated with another foreign company, Ciba-Geigy, for the exclusive marketing rights in the United States for our next product, metoprolol, I recalled the negative experiences with Warner Lambert. When I chaired the meeting to discuss the terms of the contract, I asked the representatives from Ciba-Geigy if there was a risk that there would be a conflict of interest between metoprolol and their own product, Trasicor.

We were assured that this wouldn't be the case. Trasicor had been licensed to another company in the United States. They promised to devote all their resources to metoprolol. Unfortunately that's not how it turned out. After a few years, Cibya-Geigy took back Trasicor from the licensee. They spent millions of dollars on clinical trials with their own product. They treated metoprolol differently. Before it was registered in the United States, they didn't carry out a single test on the drug they had licensed from us. The only reason that metoprolol was ever registered in the U.S., and became a major product, was because the Food and Drug Administration accepted the clinical documentation that Hässle's Medical Department produced from outside the United States.

The problems we experienced in working with both of these foreign companies illustrates the so-called NIH Syndrome. NIH stands for "Not Invented Here". Products licensed from outside the company are seen by employees as intruders. This easily turns into resistance to licensed products and a desire to prove at any price that the company's own products are better.

The Alprenolol Party was the Beginning of a New Project

It was a major event in our company's history when the first result of our research, alprenolol, was approved for use and began to be sold in many countries.

The project managers and those who had made important contributions were invited to a dinner in our guest restaurant to celebrate this milestone. That party, one evening in late October, 1967, was the starting signal for a new project that in 1975 led to an even more important breakthrough, metoprolol, sold in the U.S. as Lopressor and Toprot-XL.

At the end of the meal, Bengt Åblad burst out enthusiastically: "Now we've learned how to make an important medicine. The next one will be even better." The reason for his optimism was two discoveries made by our researchers during the alprenolol project. They were examples of the so-called "Serendipitous Discovery".

In his report to the Astra Group's research conference in 1966, Bengt Åblad had called for the creation of a beta-blocker with even better characteristics. He said research should concentrate on blockers with a more powerful effect on the heart's receptors and less effect on the receptors bronchi and the blood vessels if possible.

The Three Princes from Serendip

Serendip was the medieval Arab name for Sri Lanka, once called Ceylon.

According to an Arabian fairy tale, three princes competed for the hand of a beautiful princess of Serendip. Her father, the king, decreed that the suitor who, after a year's search, could produce the most valuable discovery, would get the princess.

When the three princes met at the castle after a year, each had remarkable things to show. They were things that must have been seen by other people but who didn't understand their true value.

When the English writer Horace Walpole read this story in 1752, he wrote a commentary. He suggested that one should call these unexpected discoveries and observations "serendipity discoveries".

In the scientific literature the term "serendipity discoveries" has come to mean two things. In the first case when someone, like the princes, sees something that others have stumbled over without realizing its value. It also has come to mean unexpected discoveries that are made when researchers are looking for a certain effect but instead find something totally different. An effect contrary to that which was expected can drive research forward in completely new directions. Two such discoveries were the impetus for the new program that in 1975 resulted in Astra's at the time greatest product, metoprolol.

In 1963, our researchers had tested the compound H35/25 in the hope of finding a beta-blocker with a strong effect on the receptors of the heart. Unfortunately, this compound had a poor effect on the heart, but had a stronger effect on the bronchi and lungs.

Such a substance in itself was of little medical interest. It would undoubtedly cause side effects in the form of breathing difficulties. What was interesting is that H35/25 in fact made Hässle famous among pharmacologists around the world. It has become a valuable tool for clarifying the different receptors in different organs.

Hässle's researchers realized at the time that they had made an important discovery. The effect of H35/25 indicated that the beta receptors were probably not the same in all organs. Those in the heart and the bronchi differed. That meant that it should be possible to develop a medicine with a specific effect on the heart or the bronchi with less risk for effects on other organs and less undesirable side effects.

But we didn't know how we could find compounds with the opposite effect of H35/25, with a stronger effect on the heart than on the bronchi. When, three years later, we found such a compound, it gave us the basis for the new project.

To strengthen alprenolol's patent protection, we synthesized a number of variations of the compound in 1966. One of them, H64/52, showed a stronger effect on the heart's receptors than in the bronchi and the blood vessels. It was an unexpected discovery that indicated where to look for a beta-blocker that primarily affected the heart.

In the new project, our goal was to produce a drug better at lowering blood pressure than alprenolol which nevertheless had been shown to be an important medicine for the treatment of high blood pressure.

Our studies had shown that a drug that was more effective in reducing blood pressure probably wouldn't have the stimulating effect that alprenolol had. The effect was certainly weak, but meant that asthma patients tolerated alprenolol better than the competing drug that lacked the stimulating effect. These two unexpected discoveries from 1963 and 1966 showed the possibility of making effective blood pressure reducing drugs with less risk of side effects for asthma patients.

Just an Effect on the Heart

H64/52 gave our chemists an indication of how the synthesis program should be set-up. During the years 1967–71 we synthesized several hundred compounds looking for an effective blood pressure reducer with the least possible effect on the bronchi and the blood vessels. We coined the phrase, heart-selective beta-blockers.

As an example of the problems facing the project, I can mention the most effective beta-blocker, H104/08. It had been the most interesting substance in the animal studies and we decided to take it to clinical trials, but in the extensive safety tests that were carried out first, it turned out that the compound caused tumours in mice, and had to be discarded.

Both of the compounds H87/07 and H93/26 met our demands for potent beta-blockers that were heart-selective and passed all the safety tests without any complaints. The compound, H93/26, which was produced in 1969, lacked the heart-stimulating effect we wanted to avoid. The other compound had a slight heart-stimulating effect, but it was more heart-selective than H93/26. We applied for patents for H87/07 and H93/26 in the Spring of 1969.

In our research group and among our consultants, there were differing opinions as to the importance of the stimulating effect so we decided to study both compounds in parallel trials and let the effect on patients determine which would become the final medicine. To work with two compounds demanded greater resources for the safety tests and the clinical trials, but we didn't see any other way to produce the ideal medicine we were seeking.

The results of the clinical trials showed that H93/26 was considerably more effective in lowering blood pressure than H87/07. From 1972 we concentrated on that compound alone.

As late as May, 1972 there were intensive discussions on the advantages and possible risks of compounds with and without a heart-stimulating effect.

The discovery by Hässle's researchers that the receptors in the heart, bronchi and blood vessels are not the same was confirmed by a research group in the United States. A publication in 1967 indicated that these scientists had independently arrived at the same conclusion. They called the heart's receptors beta-one receptors and those of the bronchi and blood vessels beta-two.

Our pharmacologist, Enar Carlsson later published a study that demonstrated that the division by different organs was not entirely correct. He maintained that there were both kinds of receptors in all organs that have what are called adrenergic receptors. However, there are mainly beta-one receptors in the heart while beta-two receptors dominate in the bronchi and blood vessels. This meant that we could not completely eliminate the effect on the bronchi and blood vessels. The differences between the organs were judged to be so great, however, that we could continue to pursue our goal of heart-selective beta-blockers.

Enar Carlsson's discovery was of great importance for research on beta receptors. His ideas attracted considerable international attention and his observations have been confirmed by other researchers. He was made manager of the new project.

Co-operation with Ciba-Geigy

During the Winter of 1969-70, we became more and more convinced that we must have better resources for the promising projects with which we were working. At the same time that we had succeeded in producing interesting compounds in our search for heart-selective beta-blockers, we also had a promising compound for a medicine to fight depression ready for testing on healthy subjects. We were also anxious to get on with the project to find a completely new ulcer medicine.

In our talks with the Group management, we tried to get our research grant increased. When this met with no response, we looked in other directions. One way to get more resources was to work with a foreign pharmaceutical company.

At that time, there was an ambition at Astra to centralize all research under a single Research Director at the Group's headquarters in Södertälje, but without the freedom we had hitherto enjoyed, we didn't think our limited resources would allow us to create the unique products we were hoping to discover.

Fortunately the Group's president, Arne Wegerfelt, still believed that Astra's research and development activities should be decentralized to the three units in Södertälje, Lund, and Mölndal and that we should continue to work with the same degree of freedom that we had previously enjoyed. The support we received from Wegerfelt's closest colleague, Sven Sundling, was without doubt of great importance in maintaining our freedom and the special climate we had built up, a research climate that we believed was a prerequisite for creativity.

Hässle's president Kjell Holmquist and I agreed that we should investigate the prerequisites for collaboration with the Swiss company, Ciba-Geigy.

Hässle had been the representative for Geigy's products in Sweden, Norway, and Finland for fifteen years. The contact provided us with a source of knowledge as well as doctors' goodwill, because of the new medicines we introduced. It was also an important source of income.

When the two companies, Ciba and Geigy decided to merge, there was a risk that we would lose the Geigy agency. We had heard how Ciba-Geigy had terminated agreements with agents in country after country in favor of their own marketing and local subsidiaries.

If we could underline the positive contributions Hässle had made as an agent for Geigy in the Nordic countries, and interest the management of the new Group in joint research, we thought we might be able to negotiate an agreement.

I asked my closest colleague Hans Corrodi to contact a friend from his student years who was then working with research at Ciba-Geigy. On the phone he tried to accertain what the reaction might be among the research management about working with us. Hans came back to me and reported that the situation appeared hopeless. His friend in Basel had heard the head of research, Professor Hugo Bein, say that our Research Director was a "Mr Pharmacist" with whom he had no interest in working.

It wasn't the first time that my lack of an academic title had been an obstacle on an international level. Particularly in the United States, contacts were much more difficult when you didn't have a Ph.D. The honorary doctorate I received from the University of Gothenburg in 1972 had a very positive effect on our collaboration with companies in Switzerland and the United States.

Hans Corrodi sounded embarrassed when he told me about the result of his query in Basel. I assured him that, when we were done, Professor Bein would be issuing us the invitation to discuss working together.

I asked our head librarian to find out everything published by Dr. Hugo Bein. The summary of his publications indicated that he had worked with adrenergic mechanisms, as well as with blood pressure medicines and psychopharmaca. When I saw this, I wrote a letter to Professor Bein: "Considering the interesting studies you've done in these fields, perhaps you would be interested in meeting our project consultants, especially Professors Arvid Carlsson, Björn Folkow, and Lars Werkö."

After a few weeks, I received a friendly letter with an invitation for Hans Corrodi and myself to visit Ciba-Geigy's research laboratories in Basel. These were impressive facilities where 3,000 researchers and technicians worked, twenty times the size of our research and development department in Mölndal.

It turned out that Ciba-Geigy's management was interested in working with us. In the Spring of 1970 a delegation headed by Professor Bein arrived in Mölndal.

Our guests from Switzerland were impressed by the research that was carried out at the Medical Faculty of the University of Gothenburg and the open collaboration we had with the researchers there. They had never seen that kind of co-operation before. They were anxious to make contact with these university researchers.

During the Summer of 1970, Kjell Holmquist and I negotiated an agreement with Ciba-Geigy which gave us the right to remain representative for the company in Sweden, Finland and Norway, and organize a joint scientific co-operation. In return Ciba-Geigy wanted the licensing rights for one of our heart-selective beta-blockers. Most of all, Ciba-Geigy wanted the rights to H93/26.

Hans-Erik Leufsted, who was responsible for the pharmaceutical division within Astra, finally agreed to work with us in drawing up the agreement with Ciba-Geigy.

The agreement went into effect on January 1, 1971. During the first few years it gave us the increased resources we had hoped for. The most important contribution was that chemists at Ciba Geigy manufactured 200 kg of H93/26, which meant that we could quickly get started with the safety tests and clinical trials in many countries.

For various reasons, Ciba-Geigy did not succeed in carrying out the international test program we had counted on which had been one of the main reasons why we had wanted to work with them. We soon discovered that their medical division was emotionally committed to the company's own beta-blocker Trasicor. At an international symposium, Ciba-Geigy's Medical Director said in a lecture that the heart-selective beta-blockers had theoretical advantages over the first generation beta-blockers to which Trasicor belonged. But, he said, no difference had been found in clinical trials.

This was before the clinical evaluation of our heart-selective compounds was finished. Had he said it was too early to express an opinion on their clinical value, we would have accepted that, but this was a signal to his employees to give priority to Trasicor over the product they had received under licence.

Here was the same "NIH" problem we had encountered with the licensing of alprenolol in the United States.

The agreement with Ciba-Geigy didn't just mean development of H93/26 to a finished medicine, it also involved closer co-operation developing medicines for heart diseases. This work gave us experience in how the Swiss pharmaceutical industry worked. We learned how Ciba-Geigy company handled patent issues. Their competence was of a completely different order than ours. We could refer to this experience when we later argued for development of the Group's competence and resources for the handling of patents.

It was also very useful to learn from Ciba-Geigy's experts about the registration of medicines and contacts with the authorities in countries where we lacked experience, such as Japan and the United States.

According to the agreement, our research co-operation would go on for seven years during the first phase after which it would be reappraised. Two years before the period ended, all of us at Hässle were in agreement that we shouldn't continue the co-operation. The primary reason was that we felt that the research conferences and decision-making at the Swiss company were far too unwieldy and bureaucratic.

151

Our researchers were used to discussing new ideas and proposals at informal meetings in the staff restaurant and on return trips from conferences. This was virtually unthinkable within the heavily centralized Ciba-Geigy. All discussions and agreements between chemists, pharmacologists and physicians had to be noted in minutes at formal meetings.

The centralized control at Ciba-Geigy reinforced my opinion that decentralized freedom is one of the most important preconditions for creativity and high productivity in research. The important medicines that the relatively small research and development organization at Hässle created illustrate the value of the motivation and fighting spirit this freedom can provide.

Another reason for our wishing to break off the co-operation was that research management in Basel seemed to be far too dependent on support from the company's marketing experts for choosing projects and deciding which compounds should be used for clinical trials.

We thought that the choice of projects should be based on medical needs, access to knowledge and the qualified personnel necessary to start meaningful work.

This means that research at an early stage should be carried out without interference from market analysts and others with experience of the products already existing in the marketplace. If research is influenced by marketing considerations at an early stage, there is a great risk that the perspective becomes too short-term.

When a project has come so far that a chosen compound has been shown to have clinical value, then it is important to have good contacts between the researchers and the company's marketing department. During the development process itself, and while extensive clinical testing programs are carried out, centralized control is extremely important. This is often the phase in which the greatest costs occur.

It is my conviction that the influence the marketing departments and economists at the major international pharmaceutical companies seem to wield over research is one of the reasons that, despite their considerable resources, they are unable to create more products based on radical innovations. In other words, completely new medicines.

The Astra Group's success during the past twenty years depends, to a large degree, on the freedom researchers at subsidiaries have enjoyed to work with university scientists. This has provided the prerequisites for the development of medicines with new active mechanisms that have met important medical needs.

Record Fast Registration

When the Swedish application for the registration of metoprolol, H93/26, was turned in to the Swedish Drug Control agency in August, 1974, the average registration period was just over two years. For metoprolol to be approved for marketing in just seven months indicates that the authorities considered the new medicine was important and the documentation of high quality. The product was registered in Sweden and a number of other countries under the brand name Seloken®, in Germany as Beloc®.

In the United States it was marketed as Lopressor® and by Astra as Toprol-XL®.

In the registration application we presented studies of 500 patients with high blood pressure, or angina pectoris, who had been treated in controlled studies with good results. The drug had been accepted well without serious side effects.

Metoprolol had certainly met our goal of creating a drug that was significantly better than the medicines that already existed.

Clinical Trials of High Quality

One reason that metoprolol has been one of the best-selling medicines in the world for fifteen years is certainly the high quality of the clinical trials that Hässle's Medical Department carried out, especially in connection with clinics at hospitals in Gothenburg. One important reason is that the clinical trials continued after the compound's registration. For several years, millions of dollars were spent on gaining knowledge of the drug's value for the long-term treatment of high blood pressure and as a medicine to reduce the risk of sudden death after a heart attack. These studies have attracted international attention.

When Gillis Johnsson was hired by Hässle in 1969, he was the first

153

physician to work in the Swedish pharmaceutical industry who had assistant professor status within the new science of clinical pharmacology. This meant a great deal for the development of professional competence within Hässle's Medical Department and for our international contacts.

Clinical pharmacology had its breakthrough in Sweden at the same time that metoprolol was being evaluated in human pharmacological and clinical tests. The first professorship in clinical pharmacology in Sweden, at the University of Linköping, was awarded to Dr. Folke Sjöquist in 1970. In 1972 he became professor at the Karolinska Institute and Chief Physician at Stockholm's Huddinge Hospital.

Research carried out by clinical pharmacologists is aimed at evaluating the effect of medical compounds and providing a basis for determining proper doses. This is done though studies on healthy human subjects and patients.

During the years that metoprolol was being evaluated in clinical studies, Gillis Johnson, Lennart Sölvell and Bengt Åblad took part in a working group that discussed how clinical trials in different areas of application should be organized. These discussions between the pharmacologist who was responsible for the drug's development, our clinical pharmacologist and a clinician at the hospital, were without doubt of great importance.

The pharmacist Jan B.A. Jansson, who worked at Hässle's Medical Department, planned and co-ordinated the international clinical trials of metoprolol in a program that, at that time, must have been the most extensive ever carried out on a Swedish drug.

Bioanalytic Chemistry

In order to determine the right dose of a drug, it is vital to be able to analyse how much of the drug is present in the patients' blood after various doses and after a certain time. It is also important to be able to study how the medicine is broken down and how it is excreted. The science that answers these questions is pharmacokinetics, the study of how the body takes up, distributes and eliminates drugs. The methods that are used have been developed by researchers and technicians within the field of bioanalytical chemistry.

During the late 60's and the 70's, Hässle probably was one of the world's leading pharmaceutical companies when it came to methods for determining the small amounts of a drug compound and its metabolic products.

It was our work with Göran Schill at the Pharmaceutical Faculty at the University of Uppsala that gave us our competence in this area. It was from his department that the researchers came who developed the methods that made it possible to analytically determine such small amounts as a few picograms of a drug. One picogram is one billionth of a milligram. Advanced methods are required to separate and determine such small amounts of a drug in blood and urine.

During the first year in Gothenburg, there was just one half-time technician to carry out the analyses of our products that were required. By the end of the 80's there were some 90 researchers and technicians working with analyses and bioanalyses. Just for the documentation of H93/26's development into the finished drug metoprolol, hundreds of thousands of analyses were carried out and one million bits of data were processed.

Metoprolol to Millions of Patients

It's estimated that during the 80's metoprolol was used by more than six million patients a day. Because of this drug they could live more active lives. Its positive effects for the treatment of high blood pressure and angina pectoris were described in many scientific journals. This quickly made metoprolol Astra's biggest product. Together with the licensees' sales, receipts reached half a billion dollars a year for several years during the 80's.

By 1993, the total number of treatments with metoprolol had reached 50 million patient years.

Today Bengt Åblad is associate professor in Applied Pharmacology at the University of Gothenburg. He works with Hässle on long-term research on medicines for cardiovascular diseases. When I discussed the project behind metoprolol with him in October, 1990, especially how our results had met our goals and expectations, he wrote the following summary:

"What was of decisive importance for metoprolol's success were the results of the extensive studies that were begun in 1975. They have convincingly demonstrated that metoprolol increases the survival rate and maintains a good quality of life for patients with cardiovascular illnesses.

"We realized in 1975 that metoprolol was a suitable tool for studying the ideas we had been ventilating since the early 60's that beta-blockers could be expected to contribute to the realization of long-term goals for the treatment of patients with cardiovascular diseases. The goal for the treatment of high blood pressure is not just to reduce the blood pressure, the important thing is to prevent fatal or disabling complications, especially heart attacks and stroke. The goal for the treatment of coronary illness by reducing the blood pressure is not just to relieve angina pectoris, the important thing is to prevent heart attacks and sudden death.

"The studies that would throw light on these long-term goals for treatment took many years and required careful planning.

"The studies with metoprolol, which be began in 1975-76, ended in 1981, 1984 and 1988. Our decision to begin this expensive long-term research was partly based on the results of two published studies, one on heart attack patients in Gothenburg, the other on patients with hypertonia in the United States.

"The work done in Gothenburg was a survival study with alprenolol that was carried out and published by Vedin, Wilhelsson and other cardiologists. It attracted international attention. The results showed that alprenolol reduced the risk of sudden death after a heart attack.

"These encouraging results motivated us to begin more extensive studies with the heart-selective beta-blocker metoprolol on patients who had suffered heart attacks.

"In 1976 a study was begun in Gothenburg under the direction of Åke Hjalmarsson, who is now Professor of Cardiology at the University of Gothenburg. Another study was carried out in Stockholm under the direction of Nina Rehnqvist and Gunnar Olsson. The results, which were published in 1981 and 1984, showed that metoprolol treatment increased the survival rate and improved the quality of life during the years following a heart attack. The number of deaths fell by a third. In addition, metoprolol reduced the risk of serious complications, such as new heart attacks and stroke."

The minutes of a consultation conference held in August, 1975 re-

156

veal that Åke Hjalmarsson made an important contribution when he carried out a study in which metoprolol was injected into patients who had suffered acute heart attacks. It turned out that metoprolol didn't just relieve the pain. The drug also seemed to protect the heart muscle and prevent the damage from spreading.

According to Bengt Åblad's summary:

"At the same time that our metoprolol studies were being carried out, several similar studies with other beta-blockers were going on in other parts of the world. The results showed that two other beta-blockers demonstrated the same positive effects that we saw with metoprolol, but studies on other beta-blockers didn't produce such positive results. This may mean that not all beta-blockers are equal where protecting the heart after a heart attack is concerned.

"Metoprolol is now used around the world for the follow-up treatment of heart attack patients."

Regarding the long-term studies of hypertonia patients, Bengt Åblad concluded:

"In 1970, the first controlled long-term study of patients with light or moderate hypertonia was published in the United States. They had primarily been treated with diuretics, drugs to increase the discharge of urine. The results showed that this treatment, which reduced blood pressure dramatically, also reduced many of the complications related to high blood pressure, including stroke attacks, but the medication hadn't prevented the most common complication, heart attacks.

"At a consultation conference in 1975, our medical advisors thought that metoprolol treatment of hypertonia patients ought to reduce the risk of heart complications more effectively than treatment with diuretics. That's why we started a study of men with uncomplicated hypertonia in 1976. Half of the patients received metoprolol and the other half diuretics. The study was led by John Wikstrand, now Professor of Cardiology at the Wallenberg Laboratory at the University of Gothenburg.

"This study included more than 3,200 patients, who were treated for up to eleven years. It showed that treatment with metoprolol had the same blood pressure reducing effect as the diuretic treatment. The two drugs had the same effect on reducing the risk of stroke. On the other hand, it was shown that treatment with metoprolol was less risky than the diuretic treatment with regard to death and invalidity caused by heart attacks and other complications connected to arteriosclerosis.

Bengt Åblad asked the question himself: "How can metoprolol extend life?"

His answer was: "The positive effects of metoprolol have in several ways confirmed the hypotheses we had in the early 60's about the possible clinical value of beta-blockers.

"We thought that a beta-blocker would be able to increase the chances of a longer life and provide a better quality of life among people with heart diseases. The reason was that these drugs ought to prevent certain negative effects of the sympathetic nervous system's stress hormones adrenaline and noradrenaline.

"During the past twenty-five years, basic research has given us important information about the function of the sympathetic nervous system. We've learned how this system contributes toward the communication between the brain and the heart, but we've also learned how the mechanisms inside individual cells are affected. Hässle's researchers have actively taken part in this work, especially regarding the effects of metoprolol.

"The results of our research indicate that the positive effect on survival can be ascribed to several factors. Besides lowering high blood pressure and relieving angina pectoris, metoprolol can counteract the process of arteriosclerosis in the arteries. Metoprolol markedly reduces the risk of sudden death caused by heart attack. This effect seems to be because of a combination of metoprolol's effect on the brain and on the heart. Hässle's studies in this area are similar to the basic research carried out at universities."

Bengt Åblad concluded his summary:

"We have found it important to carry out this cost-intensive research for two reasons. The more we learn about how a drug works, the better we can tell the doctors how it should be used in treating different illnesses. The other reason concerns Hässle's ability to contribute to creating better medicines in the future. The research involved with metoprolol gave us ideas about new and as yet untried treatment principles."

Peptic Ulcer Drugs

"The greatest Swedish discovery in modern times" was the description of the peptic ulcer medicine, omeprazol published in an article in the Stockholm daily "Dagens Nyheter" on the 25th of February, 1991. Even if it is difficult to make comparisons between different innovations, especially between drugs and work in other fields, it is obvious that omeprazol is a very useful medicine with unique properties.

When I read the article I was reminded of the often difficult struggle to keep the project alive. Particularly after our first failure in 1970, when scarcely anyone outside the project group believed in it. During the following five years I had to resort to grants from the government's Board for Technical Development and other institutions to keep the project afloat.

Five times we were told we should terminate the project, four of them during the period I was research director. That it survived despite all these set-backs is an exciting tale of dedication and the efforts of very capable scientists.

To understand what lay behind the project we have to go back to 1956 when Leif Hallberg proposed that we develop a drug to neutralize hydrochloric acid in the stomach. On that December day, we were trying to find a way to start projects that were more important medically than those we had been working with before. Hässle's Vice President, Sven-Arne Nordlindh, Marketing Director, Kjell Holmquist and I sat in a conference room at the Park Avenue Hotel in Gothenburg together with two physicians.

We had discussed the projects we were working with at the labora-

159

tory. From the list of ideas for medicines that our President, Tore Nor-lander had given me and the suggestions we had received from con-sultants, we were trying to find something that would give us more useful medicines than the drugs we already had.

"Is there really no important medical need we could satisfy?"

I had asked that question several times.

We had no resources for research that could give us a completely new kind of drug. It would be several years before we had the means to fulfil that dream. We had some competence in pharmaceutical re-search and development, even if our resources were modest. What we could do was to improve the properties of drugs that already existed. But on what should we devote our resources to find something worthwhile? Something that was really needed.

When we broke up around eleven o'clock that night we still had not come up with anything that seemed worth pursuing. It seemed im-possible to improve the standard of our current products in order to create some really beneficial new drugs.

Leif Hallberg was at that time an Associate Professor in internal me-dicine. He and I walked a few times around the statute of Poseidon in the Götaplatsen square. I then asked him one last time, "Isn't there anything that we could develop?"

Leif stopped. He finally had a suggestion. "There's an obvious need for a good liquid antacid," he said. "Patients with too much hydro-chloric acid in their gastric juices get stomach pains. They need some-thing that can quickly neutralize stomach acid. It has to have an ac-ceptable taste so patients will take it as often as they should, up to ten times a day. There isn't any good medicine right now. It's certainly a difficult problem, but that's the kind of project I think Hässle should go in for."

I was delighted about the suggestion, but when I discussed it with our marketing department I received a negative answer.

"There's already a liquid antacid. Sales only amount to 300,000 kronor (USD 40,000) a year. Even if our medicine is better, it would hardly be profitable to devote a long term development project to such a small market."

Discussions with other physicians encouraged my belief that there really was a need to develop a better antacid than those already on the market. There were tablets and a liquid acid neutralizing medicine, but none were really very effective. I was convinced that there was a need for a better medicine, and I decided to go ahead with the project.

So, when John Sjögren started at Hässle at the beginning of 1957, his first job was to develop a liquid antacid. After more than two year's work and tests, Novalucol suspension was ready for registration with the Swedish medical authorities.

Novalucol suspension, and the improved products that were developed several years later, were Hässle's best-selling product during the 60's. Sales of the Novalucol series and its successor Novaluzid still amount to around twelve million dollars a year.

The difficulty in evaluating the market for a liquid antacid is an interesting example of how you cannot judge sales opportunities and choose new products on the basis of the products that already exist. Our effort to meet an obvious medical need turned out to have been correct. Work with clinics at the University of Gothenburg demonstrated the need.

By 1965 sales of Novalucol and its improved versions had given us the ability to increase our resources for research. We thought it was reasonable to devote some of that money to the development of better medicines for ulcer patients. We had a strong desire to create something completely new, rather than merely an improvement of what already existed. Using biological-chemical research, we wanted to create a medicine using a completely new biological mechanism.

To begin with, we needed better knowledge of medical needs and ways to make contacts that could increase our competence. At Leif Hallberg's suggestion, we held a Nordic symposium in March, 1966. This symposium, called "Ulcer Illnesses", was an important milestone in Hässle's history.

The symposium taught me how common ulcers are and that there are several kinds of stomach ulcers. I also realized that there was a great need for a new type of medicine that could inhibit the secretion of hydrochloric acid in the stomach.

Ulcers

The name physicians give to sores in the stomach is ulcus ventriculi. Normally, the wall of the stomach is protected by a resistant mucous membrane. No one knows why this protection is sometimes weakened so that the hydrochloric acid and pepsin of the gastric juices can injure the stomach lining.

In mild cases one speaks of gastritis, in severe cases bleeding sores, or ulcers, can result. The main symptom is usually a pain in the stomach that hurts most below the breastbone. Sometimes the pains can extend towards the back. The patient can suddenly start to bleed and has to be taken by ambulance to hospital.

The most common ulcer is in the duodenum, the beginning of the small intestine. Called duodenal ulcers, the sores are usually found just below the lower stomach orifice. The symptoms are largely the same as in stomach ulcers, but the pains usually come later in the day, and often at night.

Irritations or sores in the lower part of the oesophagus can also cause sharp pains. An intense sore throat can be a symptom of damage in the oesophagus.

Just as the stomach is normally protected by a resistant mucous membrane, the duodenum and oesophagus are also protected by membranes. Why this protection is diminished in some people is not known for certain. Some people seem to be more disposed towards ulcers than others. Smoking and alcohol consumption can contribute. Pain relief tablets containing aspirin and other anti-inflammatory drugs can damage the membrane so that sores and bleeding occur.

Even if ulcer diseases have several causes, there is a common factor, gastric hydrochloric acid. If you reduce the supply of acid, the pain disappears and the wound can heal.

No Satifactory Remedy Existed

At the time of the symposium in 1966 there was no effective medicine for the treatment of severe ulcers which were caused by intense acid production.

In mild cases of gastritis, or peptic ulcers, the patients could find relief by changing their diet or from medicines that neutralized the hydrochloric acid. Such patients were given antacids, but even if Hässle's drug Novalucol and later Novaluzid were useful aids, they only treated the symptoms and the relief was short-lived.

For many years physicians had prescribed belladonna leaves or an extract of belladonna to reduce the production of hydrochloric acid. When science discovered how to isolate the active ingredient in belladonna, pure atropine was used. Atropine does, to some extent, reduce the production of hydrochloric acid, but it has such irritating side effects that it was difficult for patients to take the drug in effective doses.

Starting of the Project That Took 22 Years

During the symposium in March, 1966 it became obvious that there was an acute need for a completely new type of medicine for the treatment of peptic ulcers. A drug that would effectively inhibit the secretion of hydrochloric acid without the side effects of the then available drugs.

On the second day of the symposium, Lars Olbe, associate professor and Assistant Chief Physician at Gothenburg's University Hospital, summarized what had been discussed about peptic ulcer disease and its treatment. I was impressed by the research he had carried out, trying to clarify the mechanisms behind the development of ulcers.

At the dinner that concluded the symposium, I looked for Lars Olbe.

"Your summary of the discussions was very interesting," I said. "When there's a risk that as many as ten to fifteen percent of the population of our country can get ulcers, it must be essential to develop better medicines. Can't we work together? We could start a project aimed at developing a drug to inhibit the secretion of hydrochloric acid. It seems to be the most acute need."

But with a dismissing gesture Olbe replied:

"I'm not interested in working with product development. The way I see it, we know too little to start such a goal-oriented project. I want to concentrate on basic research to gain the knowledge we need."

The next day I made a request to the head of Hässle's library:

"Find out what Professor Lars Olbe has published. Give me the titles of all of his articles and copies of the summaries."

Three months after the symposium I met Lars Olbe one Saturday in his office at the hospital:

"Lars, your published papers indicate your great interest in studying the mechanisms that regulate acid secretions in the stomach.

163

You've made interesting studies on dogs and followed up results in ulcer patients, but you don't seem to have sufficient resources here at the hospital. If we can find a way to work together, Hässle could give you resources to continue your research with dogs."

This time Lars was not dismissive, but he still sounded doubtful:

"I want my research to be independent. I don't want to be a paid consultant."

I broke in immediately:

"Who said anything about your being a consultant? We just want to give you the resources to continue your research."

Now he sounded interested, but asked:

"What do you at Hässle want in return?"

Happy to note the change in his attitude, I replied "We want to look over your shoulder. To learn from your experiments with dogs. From what we learn, we want to go ahead with a goal-oriented research project."

In October, 1966 Lars Olbe began working at our research laboratory one day a week. He was assisted by the laboratory personnel. Our pharmacologist Lars Garberg learned the operation technique that Olbe used. He surgically placed a small plastic tube in a dog's stomach, a so-called stomach fistula. During the experiment gastric juices could be collected through the tube and the amount of hydrochloric acid analyzed. We could study the factors that increased and reduced the secretion of acid.

The days that Olbe was not operating or studying the fistula dogs, Lars Garberg operated. He and his colleagues who studied the effects of different drugs on the dogs' hydrochloric acid production provided important information for the project we were beginning to build up.

We had procured a number of beagles. They lived in a newly built animal department with lots of room to run around. When a dog was operated it received post-op care similar to that of human hospital patients. The dogs got used to the little plastic tubes that stuck out from their bellies, living for seven years or more with their stomach fistulas.

For these experiments, as with all animal testing, it was necessary for the staff to be close to the dogs. They had to be animal lovers and see the experiments as meaningful and important for healthcare.

When these fistula dogs were placed in a special stand while their stomach juices were tapped, they never looked upset. The animal keeper and the researchers treated the animals so well that they even went to the experiment room wagging their tails!

In the project we wanted to start, our goal was to develop a medicine with a completely new kind of mechanism. To work the way Arvid Carlsson had proposed, we needed a new biological principle around which to develop the project. Our chemists also needed a chemical lead to start with in order to set up their synthesis program.

To gather information we went through everything that had been written about ulcer diseases. The following summary is based on research papers from the 60's, along with a résumé of the history of ulcer diseases I received from Yngve Edlund and information from Lars Garberg's undergraduate thesis on ulcer diseases and their treatment at the turn of the century.

Ulcers and Their Treatment in the Past

The first physician to attribute severe vomiting and stomach pains to ulcers seems to have been the Italian Marcelle Danato. In 1597, he discovered sores in the stomach of a patient who died after much suffering.

A description of the symptoms of sores in the stomach and the duodenum was made in 1828 by the Scottish doctor, John Abercrombie. He suggested that these patients be treated with small amounts of food, primarily a milk product diet.

The concept of ulcer diseases was introduced by the French pathologist, Jean Cruveilhier in the 1830's. At that time, ulcers always meant sores in the stomach. The inclusion of sores in the duodenum, duodenal ulcers, was first established at the turn of the century.

The existence of hydrochloric acid in the stomach was first demonstrated by the Englishman, William Prout in 1824. In 1833 his countryman, William Beaumont published studies of the digestive juice secretions of an American soldier who had a stomach fistula following a bullet wound. These studies were the basis for the growing understanding of how ulcers are formed.

Gastrin is a hormone produced in the lower stomach. This hormone stimulates production of hydrochloric acid and therefore can be of importance for the formation of ulcers. The British scientist R.A. Gregory and his colleagues clarified gastrin's chemical structure in 1964.

There are a number of causes leading to the formation of ulcers. Not all the details were known when we started our project and some are still unknown. Nevertheless, there is truth to the saying "No acid, no ulcer", coined in 1910 by Karl Schwartz. During the 1940's, this was modified by Dragstedt, who said that it is an excessively high level of acid production that is harmful.

Bed rest and fasting followed by a strict diet was the only treatment for ulcers during most of the 19th century and the first half of the 20th. Doctors began trying acid neutralizing remedies, antacids, on mild cases. At the end of the 19th century bicarbonate of soda and chalk began to be used to ease the discomfort. When better antacids such as Novalucol became available in the early 60's, these medicines were used more and more.

Belladonna leaves were first used in the early 19th century to reduce the production of gastric juices. An extract of belladonna was available at Swedish pharmacies from the end of the last century and during the first half of this century. Physicians were aware, however, that belladonna contains a powerful poison. Linneus gave the plant the name Atropa belladonna after the goddess of Fate, Atropos, who cut the thread of life.

The name belladonna indicated the plant's ability to make women more beautiful by enlarging their pupils. The effect on the eyes clouded the vision of patients who had been given a dose of the extract to ease their stomach pain. The same dose caused dryness of the mouth and other side effects. The reason that researchers were unable to develop variants of belladonna's active ingredient, atropine, that was free of side effects, despite many years of effort, may be because the receptors of the signal substance acetylcholine are found in many organs.

In the stomach, acetylcholine increases the production of hydrochloric acid. The substances that counteract the effect of acetylcholine on the acid in the stomach, anticholinergics, have a negative effect on other organs where acetylcholine is also a signal substance, such as the saliva glands and the eyes.

Since there was no effective medicine for the treatment of ulcers, surgery was tried. The aim was to either remove the parts of the stomach that stimulate hydrochloric acid production or to sever the nerves that regulate acid secretion.

166

The first successful stomach operation was carried out by the Viennese surgeon, Billroth in 1881 when he operated on a woman who had cancer. The procedure he used received the name Billroth I. A year later this method was used by another surgeon on an ulcer patient. When the report on the successful operation was published, one disgruntled colleague wrote that while this was the first ulcer operation, he hoped it would also be the last. This is one of many examples of how anything new in science and medicine is met by doubts and criticism.

During the 70's and 80's the need for operations for stomach and intestinal ulcers diminished thanks to the effective medicines developed by scientists at several pharmaceutical companies. Two important drugs were created by English researchers at the companies Smith Kline & French and Glaxo.

Independently of these research groups, Hässle's scientists, working together with the Gothenburg University Hospital's Lars Olbe, developed the drug omeprazol, which was approved by the Swedish medical authorities in 1988. It has since been used in more than eighty countries.

Before our researchers found the trail that led to omeprazol, we suffered a series of major failures, setbacks and demands for the project's termination.

The Gastrin Project

When Lars Olbe observed our efforts to find the mechanisms that regulate acid production in the stomach using fistula dogs he became interested in working with us in a goal-oriented project aimed at developing a new medicine.

He held a lecture at Hässle on the mechanisms that control the secretion of hydrochloric acid in the stomach and how one might influence them.

Hydrochloric acid is produced in what are called parietal cells in the stomach's mucous membrane. The acid produced is so acidic, with a pH around 1, that the stomach would soon be eaten away if there was no protective membrane.

The production of hydrochloric acid by the parietal cells is controlled by several mechanisms and undoubtedly, not all are as yet

167

known. One way to reduce the amount of hydrochloric acid is to block the receptors on the parietal cells that receive the signals from acetylcholine, the cholinergic receptors. But since researchers at several companies had worked on that problem for many years without success, there was no point in our pursuing it.

Following Gregory's discovery of the structure of gastrin and its effects on acid secretion, the British drug company, ICI sought to develop substances similar to the gastrin molecule. The idea was that they would block the receptor that receives signals from the gastrin and in that way prevent the hormone from stimulating the parietal cells to produce hydrochloric acid.

Despite synthesizing nearly one thousand substances over a period of several years, ICI was unsuccessful in developing a useful medicine.

Lars Olbe mentioned that local anaesthetics had been shown to reduce the production of hydrochloric acid. The probable reason was because the anaesthetic inhibited the release of gastrin. However, neither lidocain nor other local anaesthetics were suitable to use as medicines. These drugs are mildly alkaline and combine with acids to produce salts. In an acidic stomach, they had little or no effect.

Olbe suggested that the first goal of our project should be to try to develop a local anaesthetic that would work in an acidic environment if this was possible. Such substances ought to inhibit the release of gastrin and in that way reduce the production of hydrochloric acid.

John Sjögren was interested in Olbe's idea. He discussed the problem with Arne Brändström whose research had shown that he could create local anaesthetics with widely divergent characteristics.

To start the project, an entirely new area had to be built up at Hässle. We also had to develop new methods for animal experiments to test the substances the chemists would be synthesizing.

Other drug researchers had tested the effects of acid secretion on rats. The methods used were rather simple, but Lars Olbe told us that rats have unusual gastric juices, and the mechanisms for the production of gastric juices seem to work in a completely different way in rats than in dogs and humans. For that reason Olbe advised us to avoid using rats as test animals. Unfortunately, we persisted since many publications described interesting experiments with rats. Finally Olbe gave in, although with great reluctance. It turned out that the experiments with rats led us on a false trail for the first three years of the project.

An animal physiologist, Bengt Wilander, was employed. Under Lars Garberg's direction, he worked out a method to test acid secretions in rats.

To the delight of our chemists and pharmacologists, some of the first substances tested gave positive results. Gradually the researchers found a connection between changes in chemical structure and biological effects.

After a couple of months, an interesting discovery was made. Some substances were effective in inhibiting hydrochloric acid secretion although they lacked a local anaesthetic effect. We believed this indicated that we might be on the trail of a completely new mechanism.

The project then concentrated on developing an as effective acid secretion inhibitor as possible without a local anaesthetic effect.

By November, 1966 we had a compound called H68/51 that seemed to be promising, which we wanted to test on healthy human subjects. Primarily we needed evidence that the results we had obtained in rats could be repeated in humans and could guide us in finding a drug effective in decreasing acid secretion in patients.

We carried out various safety tests on H68/51, including looking for possible side effects and toxicity. Unfortunately, it turned out that H68/51 was harmful to dogs' livers. No harmful effects had been observed in rats, but we obviously couldn't test the compound on humans.

Chemist Ulf Junggren, who for more than fifteen years was primarily responsible for the project's drug synthesis program, developed a new group of substances which the chemists called carbamates. These compounds were not expected to cause liver damage.

For the next two years Ulf Junggren's group synthesized 250 compounds of the carbamate type. In February 1968, the compound H81/58 was chosen for human trials.

After comprehensive safety tests on rats and dogs, an application was sent to the Swedish medical authorities seeking permission to test H81/58 on healthy human subjects. Lars Garberg and I contacted Professor Åke Liljestrand, who was responsible for drug regulation.

Since it was the first time we planned to test a substance with a completely new mechanism on humans, we were anxious to discuss the project's goals and comment on the discoveries we had made testing the substance on different animals.

Liljestrand underlined the clear medical need for the type of medicine we were aiming at. Our application was granted and we were given permission to test H81/58 on human subjects.

We began with very small doses. When the dosages were increased we discovered in one test person a change in the blood that might indicate an effect on the liver. The tests were broken off. Unfortunately we were unable to test the effect of the compound on acid secretion in humans. We still didn't know if we were on the right track and we had no confirmation that the tests on rats were giving us reliable results.

This negative result gave the company management doubts about our work. While research was still being carried out with very small resources, it had been granted project status. The first year it had been classified as exploratory research. Within the framework of our research and development budget, we had the right to use a certain amount, usually ten per cent, for free research. It was within this framework that we started the project.

Going through all the test results, we found another compound that was so different in chemical structure from H81/58 that we had reason to believe that it would not have the same side effects. It was called H81/75 and had first been synthesized as early as April, 1968.

We carried out all the safety tests on the substance and there were no indications of harmful effects. The compound had displayed very good results in tests done on rats. It had more or less completely inhibited acid secretion, so we had great expectations for H81/75.

Lars Olbe suggested we test the compound on fistula dogs. We did find an effect, but it was very weak.

A new application was submitted to the authorities. We received permission to test the substance on healthy human subjects.

When H81/75 was tested on humans in increasing doses, no signs were found of side effects. It was well tolerated by the body. So far so good. The Big Moment we had been waiting for for three years had arrived. We looked for evidence that our drug actually inhibited stomach acid secretion in humans. Unfortunately it turned out that the substance had no effect at all on humans. Not even in doses that were far larger than the doses which had given very positive results in rats measured in milligrams of drug per kilogram of body weight.

But, despite our great disappointment, we still didn't want to abandon the project.

Now we had evidence that the rat model was unsuitable for testing human acid secretion. Lars Olbe had certainly been right. We stopped working with rats and began testing acid secretion in fistula dogs.

The most serious problem was that we had absolutely no idea what chemical structure we should use as a starting point for synthesizing new substances since it had been shown that the carbamates had no effect on humans.

"Terminate the Project!"

When our negative results were presented at the Astra Group's annual research conference in the Fall of 1970, we were firmly advised to terminate the project. The professors on the board's Science Council and the other members of the Research Council were unanimous in their recommendation.

Everyone spoke against the project. The substances we had chosen for tests were either toxic, had potential side effects, or had absolutely no effect on humans. We had no new chemical structure from which to start our renewed effort. It was easy to find arguments to end the project.

But with the support of Lars Olbe and the Hässle scientists, I insisted that the project should proceed. The primary reasons were:

– that there was still no effective drug for the treatment of peptic ulcers. The need for a new medicine was great, and

– that during the four years we had carried out this research, we had gained so much knowledge that we considered ourselves well-prepared to initiate a new project.

The strongest reason for me wanting to continue was, however, a conversation with Professor R.A. Gregory in September, 1967. Lars Olbe had invited Gregory to lecture at the University of Gothenburg. We took the opportunity to discuss our problems with him presenting our aims and how we were trying to find an acid secretion inhibitor.

Naturally, Gregory couldn't give us any guarantees, but I never forgot his final comment:

"As long as Lars Olbe is part of the project, you should have a reasonable chance of succeeding."

Group management accepted with some reluctance the continuation of the project as exploratory work. This meant that, with a reduced budget, we would be trying to discover a new biological principle and a completely new chemical structure. Certainly a difficult situation.

Somehow I had to get more funds for our research. The small allocation we had for exploratory work wasn't enough.

Thanks to Professor Arvid Carlsson's and our deputy research director Hans Corrodi's contacts with a scientist at the American pharmaceutical company, Abbott we were visited by their research director and his assistant in the summer of 1970. They were interested in collaborating with us, having noted in the scientific literature the many new chemical substances with the "H" that stood for Hässle. They were primarily interested in obtaining a licence for our beta-blocker heart medicines, but we already had an agreement with Ciba-Geigy, which gave them exclusive licensing rights for these substances in the United States and some other markets. So I suggested collaboration on the ulcer project instead.

During negotiations in Chicago we worked out an agreement covering collaboration on the project. Abbott would assign a group of chemists to the task of synthesizing substances which we would test on fistula dogs. With the chemists of two companies working on the chemical problem in different ways, we hoped to find an interesting chemical structure much faster.

Besides participation in the project, Abbott would also pay us 50,000 dollars a year to support our biological research.

If we were successful in reaching our goal of a useful patent-protected drug, Abbott would have the exclusive right to sell it in the United States and several other countries. I also came up with the idea that the royalties Abbott should pay us would increase on a sliding scale with increased sales.

Abbott's Sales Director looked very confused since the usual practice is to pay lower royalties for higher sales. My main argument was that a very high sales volume would demonstrate the value of the drug. Besides, high sales with high profitability would tolerate higher royalties. The argument was accepted. We used the same principles when we negotiated with Ciba-Geigy for the licensing of the heart medicine metoprolol.

172

The Acid Secretion Project

Thanks to the agreement with Abbott, the project could continue, but after our first failure, the name was changed from the Gastrin Project to the Acid Secretion Project. When Bengt Wilander left Hässle in 1968, animal physiologist Lars Palmer was employed to direct the project's pharmacological tests, taking over responsibility from the beginning of 1969. Working with Lars Olbe, he gained experience in using fistula dogs to test various reference substances.

Although Lars Palmer was a capable head for the biological part of the project, I discovered that his main interest was not in animal experiments. His attention was most attracted when data from the experiments was ready for processing and the statistical significance could be calculated. When I went into his laboratory to see the latest trial results, Lars was most often crouched in front of a calculator carrying out complicated calculations.

When I asked Lars Palmer if he would be interested in starting a department for processing the results of the biological tests using computers and modern data processing, his face lit up. He soon taught himself what he needed to know to buy and program suitable computers.

During the years that followed, Lars Palmer built up a well-run department with millions of dollars worth of computers. He and some of his colleagues developed a data system that greatly eased the work of the pharmacologists, chemists and analysts.

To succeed Lars Palmer as head of the project's biological research, we hired assistant professor Sven-Erik Sjöstrand, a veterinarian with a post-graduate degree in pharmacology. Between 1965 and 1971 he had worked with the chemists at the pharmaceutical company Recip, testing many different drugs. Sven-Erik had an expressed interest in studying the active mechanisms in animal experiment methodology.

In the spring of 1971, Sjöstrand began working at our pharmacological laboratory where he took part in the project developing heart and blood pressure medicines. He also took part in the psychopharmacology project and worked on the compound that became zemilidin, a drug to treat mental depression.

Sven-Erik Sjöstrand was project manager from the summer of 1972, responsible for the acid secretion project and, for the first time, Lars Olbe had a partner who spoke the same biological language. When

173

I saw these two scientists working together, I understood that the most important prerequisite for a smooth collaboration between university researchers and industry's scientists has to be a mutual respect for each others' scientific competence. The collaboration must rest on a strong common interest in reaching the intended goals and the means of reaching those goals. Another important factor, of course, is whether the "personal chemistry" works.

In a discussion in February, 1989 Peder Berntsson, who between 1970 and 1988 was head of Hässle's chemical research and responsible for the chemical side of the acid secretion project, expressed clearly his opinion of Sven-Erik Sjöstrand's contributions:

"Sven-Erik accomplished three major feats in this complicated project. The first was developing a screening method for substances that was so good that it led Chemistry to a new group of compounds that we now call benzimidazols. The second was to manage the project to the creation of H168/68, which became the unique medicine, omeprazol. The third contribution was that he understood the importance of the difficult findings of the toxicological studies that threatened to stop the project and he could interpret them correctly."

The Hunt for a New Mechanism

In the summer of 1972, work on the project intensified. Ulf Junggren, Sven-Erik Sjöstrand and Lars Olbe formed a very creative group which produced many useful inventions. The story of how this led to the peptic ulcer medicine omeprazol is an interesting example of how researchers can overcome difficulties and struggle to solve apparently impossible problems

By studies of the scientific literature, going through patent publications and visiting scientific meetings, the researchers sought clues for substances that might have an effect on acid secretion. We hoped to find a chemical structure that could serve as a starting point for a synthesis program.

As early as 1967, Ulf Junggren had seen a publication from the American company Searle. It described a number of substances with a new chemical structure which in animal trials had inhibited the secretion of hydrochloric acid. He synthesized one of these "Searle substances" in

October, 1967. It was called H75/65. It failed to arouse any interest among the researchers, however, and was never mentioned in the reports to me, since all interest was concentrated on the then exciting carbamates.

A few years later, the discovery of this interesting "Searle substance" became very important for the project, but at the time it was quite simply forgotten. At Searle these substances hadn't resulted in any drugs and the project ended there when the findings were published. But for us at Hässle, this substance would eventually take us towards our goal in an unexpected way.

At the beginning of 1972, Lars Palmer visited a pharmacology congress in Budapest. In his report he mentioned that at one lecture he heard that a compound called CMN131 had shown a capacity to inhibit acid secretion. The French company Servier had developed a number of substances, among them CMN131, in the hope of finding a drug to treat infections. Since CMN131 was reported to be too toxic for tests on humans, Palmer hadn't thought it worth bringing to the attention of the project group.

The remarkable thing was that the chemical structure of CMN131 showed similarities with the "Searle substance" with our name H75/65, created five years earlier.

As Peder Berntsson described it in February, 1989:

"One day in the spring of 1972, Lars Palmer and I were cycling home from work. He happened to mention CMN131. I was interested, so I synthesized it, but it didn't arouse any interest in the project group."

Later, I asked Sven-Erik Sjöstrand when CMN131 had actually gotten us onto a new trail.

"When I took over responsibility for the project in 1972," he told me, "I went through the notes and minutes of meetings from the previous years. In Palmer's report from the congress in Budapest, I found notes about CMN131 indicating that it had an acid inhibiting effect. What I found particularly interesting was that the same substance was among the "Searle substances". Moreover, CMN131 had been synthesized by Peder, but oddly enough had never been tested by Hässle. This might have been because, at that point, we were unsure which test methods to use. When I tested CMN131 on our fistula dogs, I found that it was an effective acid secretion inhibitor.

"We finally had a clue. CMN131 became one of the most important reference substances in tests and the starting point for our entire new synthesis program. Ulf Junggren and I had lively discussions about how we would set up the program. Beginning in the Fall of 1972, things really got going."

Sven-Erik Sjöstrand improved the fistula method on the dogs so that it was more suitable for indicating the best substances. He also developed other test methods.

During a visit to a research group in the United States, Sven-Erik Sjöstrand learned how to treat the stomach membrane of frogs to study acid secretion. He used the same technique in our laboratory, using instead the stomach membrane from guinea pigs.

Our workshop built a device in which small pieces of stomach mucous membrane were placed in a nutrient solution. For an entire day, the membrane sections could be stimulated to produce hydrochloric acid. By connecting the device to a computer, the stimulation and the analysis of the hydrochloric acid which was produced could be completely automated. This method became a useful tool for studying the mechanisms for inhibiting acid secretions.

It was also an interesting alternative to traditional animal testing.

We Weren't Alone

At the same time that our peptic ulcer project moved in this new direction in 1972–73, we also discovered that we weren't alone in our research field. Publications from the American pharmaceutical company, Smith Kline & French (SK&F), described how at their British research center, pharmacologist James Black had started a project with basically the same goals as ours: to develop a medicine to inhibit acid secretion using a completely new mechanism.

Ironically, Hässle and the British researcher had been rivals before. In the early 60's Black had developed the beta-blocker, Inderal for the British company ICI. After competing in the quest to find a new medicine for heart diseases, we were now both searching for a new way to treat peptic ulcers.

In 1964, two years before we began our project, Black had gotten SK&F interested in starting a project with an interesting working hypothesis. It had long been known that histamine stimulates gastric secretions.

However, histamine affects several organs in the body. As early as 1948, Björn Folkow had published studies which showed that there were two different receptors which were sensitive to histamine. He had made this discovery while studying the effect of histamine on blood pressure.

James Black succeeded in identifying the receptor which he called the H2-receptor. After several years, Black's research group found burinamide which blocked the H2-receptors in the parietal cells in the stomach. They had succeeded in developing a compound that inhibited acid secretion with a new mechanism.

But burinamide was too weak. Within a year the British scientists had produced a much more effective compound called metiamide. Unfortunately, the clinical tests indicated that this drug caused side effects and metiamide was set aside.

Black has since related that the SK&F management, at that point, began to have serious doubts about the project. There was a great risk it would be ended, but because of Black's stubborn belief in the project's goals and potential, he succeeded in convincing his management that the project should continue.

After synthesizing and testing another 700 compounds, Black found cimetidine, which was later sold as the medicine Tagamet®. It was a great success and for several years Tagamet was the number one selling drug on the world market.

When Black was rewarded with the Nobel Prize in 1988 for Tagamet and other contributions, he described his own role in the project:

"Two things are certain. That I was there and that I couldn't have done it alone."

However, one more thing is also certain. Black had considerably more resources at his disposal when he developed first Inderal and then Tagamet, than we had at Hässle during the 60's and 70's, when we developed the beta blockers, alprenolol and metroprolol, along with the compound which became the peptic ulcer medicine, omeprazol.

That we, with relatively small resources, succeeded in developing medicines that could hold their own against those for which Black won the Nobel Prize depended to a great extent on the unique collaboration we established with university researchers.

Naturally, the discovery of the H2 blockers affected us at Hässle. When the first published reports appeared our situation was precarious. We were stuck, and there were demands for the project to be terminated. We had no new working hypothesis that could lead us to a new mechanism for inhibiting acid secretion. According to our project directives, our new medicine had to be better than Tagamet if we were to market it.

There were lively discussions within the company. Should we end the project? There were several proposals that we should develop a new H2 blocker with better properties than Tagamet. The argument was that it would be better to develop a sure thing rather than continue with our current, fumbling efforts. Perhaps we could be the second company on the world market with a H2 blocker.

Several companies have subsequently devoted major resources to this new research field. Those who thought it would be better for us to end our own project and concentrate on H2 blockers were probably more realistic than we optimists who persisted in continuing in the hope that we would find something better than the H2 blockers.

A few years after the discovery of Tagamet, the British company Glaxo succeeded in developing the H2 blocker rantidine which under the name of Zantac was a great success. Sales have been even greater than those of Tagamet. Considering the unbelievably large resources Glaxo devoted to the project, we would hardly have been able to compete had we chosen that path.

There were other reasons why we didn't concentrate on H2 blockers. For example, we knew there were H2 receptors in other organs than the stomach, such as the heart. There could be a risk of undesirable side effects in those organs.

In our project, we wanted to find a medicine that acted within the cells that produce hydrochloric acid. That would mean the least possible risk of side effects, but that also meant that we had to find a completely new mechanism.

It was a bold goal for such a small group. Black and his colleagues synthesized 2,000 compounds before they found their drug. We didn't have anything like the kind of resources they had at their disposal.

We synthesized Tagamet and used it as a reference in our tests. We wanted to be certain that the new medicine we found met our aim of being better than all others.

178

The New Road

The compound CMN131 could not be tested on humans because it was too toxic, it could have dangerous side effects. We believed that this toxicity was due to a sulfur atom in the molecule and the way it was linked to a carbon atom with what is called a double bond. The chemists tried, in different ways, to change the structure to eliminate the risk of side effects.

In an attempt to increase the efficacy of the compound as an acid secretion inhibitor, the molecule was linked to histamine. We knew that histamine is attracted to the parietal cells. We hoped that compounds which included a part of the histamine structure would be more effective than the original compounds.

In a summary of the project sent to me by Sven-Erik Sjöstrand in March, 1991, he described how the project group sought new chemical structures:

"Together with the chemists, we developed compounds based on the chemical structures of all possible compounds that in one way or another were connected with hydrochloric acid secretion and with the acid producing cells. One of these was benzimidazol, which was known to be the link between the intrinsic factor (from the parietal cells) and vitamin B12.

"Our chemists produced our first strong acid secretion inhibitor following these principles in October, 1972. It was called H77/67. It was the twenty-seventh compound we produced after we began using CMN131 as our starting point.

"After synthesizing a further 142 compounds, in June, 1973 we made a compound of crucial importance to the project. H124/26 was a benzimidazol derivative, with a basic structure that later led us to our goal, the drug omeprazol, marketed as Losec."

In April, 1981, Ulf Junggren wrote down his impressions of how the project evolved during the years he was responsible for the synthesis program. This was a year or so before this capable researcher tragically died after a short illness. In his account, he talked about synthesis on what he termed, "The New Road":

"During the hectic years of 1973 and 1974 I think we were, at most, twelve chemists in the group 'spitting' out compounds as if we were working on an assembly line. We varied the two hetero-cyclic ring

179

systems as well as the chain between them, creating around 200 compounds."

To understand the great effort made by this small group of researchers, it is important to know that every new chemical compound, every substance that was tested, was the result of several steps of synthesis. Five or six intermediate products had to be synthesized before the sought after substance could be produced. In some cases ten intermediate stages were needed. This means that thousands of new chemical compounds were created during the two years 1972 and 1973. That was when our fundamental chemical inventions were made and patented.

Ulf Junggren was certainly responsible for one of the most important contributions to the project.

Drama in Budapest

The compound H124/26 was thought to be so interesting that we wanted to study its effect on healthy human subjects as soon as possible in order to go on to clinical tests on patients.

In order to carry out the necessary safety tests, many kilograms of H124/26 were produced. When the safety studies were underway, one of our chemists discovered that a Hungarian pharmaceutical company had applied for a patent for the same compound. There was no information about effects on acid secretion. The compound had been synthesized to develop a medicine to treat tuberculosis.

When I wrote to the Hungarian company, Egyesult, we were invited to come to Budapest to negotiate for either a license under their patent or to buy the patent.

In March, 1974 our deputy research director, Lars G. Nilsson, Astra's contact for Hungary Heinz Heiwinkel and I flew to Budapest. To travel from Sweden through Austria to Hungary then was like arriving at a well-guarded concentration camp. A number of armed guards at several control stations demanded to see our passports, visas and customs documents. There was a lot of red tape.

We were not allowed to negotiate with Egyesult. The responsible state organization, Medimpex took charge of the discussions completely. Egyesult's research director and the company's patent specialist were in the room where the talks were held, but they were never allowed to take part in the discussions.

We had to wait a long time for the representative from Medimpex to show up. He turned out to be a short man who apparently tried to look taller by walking on his toes. He was looking at the ceiling when he came into the room and almost stumbled on the threshold. He began by explaining to us how really valuable their patent was. Despite this, he was willing to license it to us, or let us buy it, but the terms had to be generous.

We offered Medimpex three alternatives: A high one-time payment without royalties, a lower one-time payment plus a low royalty on future sales of the medicine we hoped to develop, or no payment, but twice as large royalties for future sales.

Medimpex choose the second alternative. After four hours of discussions about the size of the initial payment and the royalties, we reached an agreement. They asked us to write a draft agreement.

With the help of a secretary at our hotel during the evening, we wrote the basis for the agreement in the form of minutes from the day's discussions.

The next morning was a replay of the previous day. Together with the head of research from Egyesult, we three Swedes had to wait a long time for the short man from Medimpex to stumble over the threshold into the conference room. He made no attempt to apologize for making us wait long after the agreed upon time.

Our host read through our draft minutes with the terms we had agreed upon the previous day. Then he began again to talk about how valuable the patent was. Applications had been filed in many countries. To receive such comprehensive patent protection was certainly worth a lot of money. His superiors could not accept the low one time payment we had offered. We had to offer much better terms. He argued heatedly for higher compensation. Then the telephone rang at the other end of the large conference room.

While the Medimpex representative was talking on the telephone we could see him begin to droop. When he was finished, he called over the research director from Egyesult. When the two Hungarians returned to the table, they sat quietly a few moments. The man from Medimpex looked crushed when he virtually whispered:

"No patent. The applications have been withdrawn everywhere.

No patent fees have been paid."

The research director, who had not said a word either day, took his pipe out of his mouth, rose to his feet, and just said "Auf Wiedersehn!" Then he hurried out of the room.

Neither the research director nor the company's patent expert had been told about the decision to withdraw the patent applications. High level politicians in the party dictatorship had decided over their heads.

None of us said anything for a moment. Finally I asked our host, "Could you please call for a taxi?"

A New Setback

We waited excitedly for the results of the safety tests of H124/26. Finally we would be able to test a truly promising compound on humans!

Our American partner, Abbott carried out these safety tests. Our budget was so little we couldn't afford the expense. We were very disappointed when Abbott's research director called and reported that they had found toxic effects on rats.

We couldn't test H124/26 on human subjects. Once again we didn't know if we were on the right trail. We had no proof that our substances had any effect on humans.

When we reported the negative results of the safety tests to the Group's annual research conference we were once again urged to terminate the project.

At the same time we could report on an interesting observation that had been made during the safety tests. H124/26 had been converted into another chemical compound in the test animals' livers, what is called a metabolite. This turned out to be a much more active acid secretion inhibitor than H124/26. It was no easy task to ascertain the metabolite's chemical structure and then synthesize it. We called it H83/69 and it turned out to be one of the important milestones on the road to our goal.

H83/69, which was synthesized in February, 1974, was the 340th substance we synthesized and tested in the project. This compound had a much stronger effect than H124/26 and it differed from H124/26 in that it had an oxygen atom bound to the sulfur atom. This

182

group of chemical compounds is called sulfoxides. It was a completely new compound which moved the project forward in an unexpected way, since these sulfoxides were much more effective than any of the substances we had previously synthesized.

At the research conference it was impossible not to be impressed by the persistency with which our researchers came to grips with each new problem that appeared. We were given one more year to show a positive result.

The initial safety studies with H83/69 looked promising. Again we hoped we had chosen the substance that would be a valuable medicine.

Side Effects on the Thyroid Gland and the Immune System

In the Fall of 1974, I had the embarrassing task of reporting to the Group's annual research conference that H83/69 had shown to give undesirable effects on the thyroid gland and the thymus, which is involved in the body's immune system. Such a substance could obviously not be tested on humans, even if no other toxic effects were observed in the tests on rats and dogs over a long period.

But we had no plans to give up. Our researchers had worked out a program to clarify the reasons for these effects on the thyroid and the thymus. When I argued for a continuation of the project, one of the professors on the board's scientific council said it seemed as if we always found toxic effects. Perhaps, he said, the acid secretion inhibiting effect was the result of the substance's toxicity. In that case, it was meaningless to continue.

After much debate, I finally got the research council to accept that we could spend one more year working on these problems which were deemed to be of scientific interest, but that was to be the project's last reprieve.

Within the project group, of course, we were quite concerned about having just one year to reach a positive result. Otherwise we would have to terminate the project.

The animal experiment model needed to minimize the toxic effects on the thyroid and thymus was developed by Torbjörn Malmfors, then head of Astra's safety laboratory, and the pathologist Niilo Havu, together with project manager, Sven-Erik Sjöstrand.

Through an incredibly skilful and elegant research effort our chemists and pharmacologists solved this difficult toxicological problem. Fifty new substances were tested using the screening model that was developed. It was discovered that there was a connection between the fat-solubility of the substances and their effect on the thyroid gland.

Sven-Erik Sjöstrand was involved in a real detective hunt when he searched through the literature for substances that had an effect on the thyroid. He knew that medicines that are used to treat goitre act on the thyroid gland and suggested that we test compounds called thiouracils. Sjöstrand found that these drugs had certain similarities to H83/69. Finally, he found a publication that explained how a research group had succeeded in changing the chemical structure of thiouracils so that the effect varied from a powerful action on the thyroid to none at all.

This was what we needed to solve our problem. Through a patience-straining program of synthesis and testing the researchers succeeded in completely removing the undesired effects on both the thyroid and the thymus.

This complicated research effort took far more than the one year reprieve we had received to find positive results, but the scientific result was impressive, and once again we were allowed to continue.

In December, 1976, we developed the compound H149/94. It was a much more effective acid secretion inhibitor than anything we had previously tested. It was completely free of any effects on the thyroid or the thymus. Nor could we find any other undesirable effects. Finally, we felt sure we were near our goal.

We quickly prepared to put H149/94 through the necessary safety tests and tests on healthy human subjects so we could hopefully go on to clinical tests on ulcer patients. Finally, after a ten year struggle, we seemed to be approaching our goal.

The Agreement with Abbott is Ended

Not one of the substances that Abbott's chemists had synthesized during four years had shown any effect on acid secretion in our tests. The researchers in our group became more and more negative about working with our American partner.

184

We never felt any real interest from Abbott's side when the research groups of the two companies met every six months in the US or Sweden. There was none of the fighting spirit that we were used to. The Americans seemed only to be going through the motions, following a set routine without thinking. They synthesized a certain number of chemical compounds according to our agreement, but Abbott's chemists seemed to lack the drive to create something really unique at any price, though their resources were far greater than ours. Their research director was positive and wanted to continue working with us, but that was of little help when their chemists were so uninterested.

The only meaningful contribution Abbott made was to help us with the safety tests for H124/26. The interesting metabolite they found then had moved the project forward.

When Abbott wanted to reduce their research grant, I flew to Chicago to discuss our collaboration with the company management.

Their attitude towards the project was far from positive. During a dinner their research director tried to support me and spoke out in favor of an increased stake in the project, but the President of Abbott's Pharmaceutical Division was against continued participation. He said the company's market analysts had determined that Abbott's sales of the product we hoped to develop could not possibly exceed fifteen million dollars from its third year on the market and after two years of promotion. There was no interest in a long term investment in such a project. We hadn't even demonstrated that we were on the right trail to our goal. The division president said we could hardly hope for any result in the near future.

I tried to argue that the medical need for a completely new peptic ulcer medicine was so great that Abbott could count on a much larger market. More likely, the company's third year sales would reach a hundred million dollars.

At that point, the division president lifted his wine glass and turning to his marketing director at the other end of the table he said:

"Listen to this optimist. He thinks he knows the American market. He thinks our sales of this product they hope to develop will be a hundred million dollars by the third year. Let's toast to that optimism!"

General merriment broke out around the table.

A few years later, if I had run into that division president, I would have been able to say:

"I was wrong, it didn't take three years. Abbott could have had a hundred million dollars in sales for our ulcer medicine in the very first year!"

By then, the American company SK&F had produced Tagamet, which in its first year had sales of 98 million dollars in the United States alone. A figure which soon doubled.

Omeprazol, the final result of our project, was better than Tagamet in several ways and should have reached the same sales figures.

Here, once again, is an example of how difficult it is for marketing analysts and economists to evaluate a completely new product, an innovation. Sales opportunities are usually judged on the basis of products already on the market. In this case, Abbott probably studied the sales of the various peptic ulcer medicines sold in the United States at the time. Perhaps they included a slight increase based on the assumption that our medicine would be better than already existing products. But they clearly had difficulty realizing that a completely new principle could create new avenues for the treatment of ulcers and in that way would create a larger market.

The project group and Hässle's management agreed that we should cancel our agreement with Abbott. We did this in May, 1974. Had we not done so, we would have been required to give Abbott licensing rights for omeprazol in the United States and a number of other markets.

But in cancelling the agreement, we also lost the grant from our American partner at a time when we still very much needed the money to continue the project.

The Government Saves the Project

In the early 70's, Sweden's Board for Technical Development started a commission for drug research. It was chaired by Professor Einar Stenhagen from the University of Gothenburg. He was a stimulating leader, interested in supporting complicated research projects which had close contacts with basic research.

As soon as we decided to end the agreement with Abbott, I sent an application to the board asking for a grant of more than 300,000 dollars for the project. We received around 250,000 dollars to spend over a two year period. That carried us into 1976. The sole condition for the grant was that the company also invested at least as much in the project.

Because of this condition, the grant didn't just save the project from termination. It also meant that we had more money for our research than ever before.

When omeprazol was approved for marketing in 1988, the board received its money back, with interest. That amounted to 500,000 dollars. For a project that, in 1988's monetary terms, was estimated to 170 million dollars, that wasn't a very large sum. But without that crucial government grant, the project probably wouldn't have survived at all.

When I wrote to the board's general director to tell him how much the grant meant to us, he replied by sending me a copy of the letter with the signatures of all the board's staff all expressing their pleasure that one of their grants had been so important in helping a Swedish company develop a major export product.

The Compound's Further Destiny

After the animal experiments and safety tests on H149/94, we were convinced that we had developed a very interesting substance which was given the name picoprazol. We were anxious to go into studies on healthy human subjects and then continuing on to clinical tests as soon as possible.

But in June, 1978 we received a report from Astra's safety laboratory saying that when testing picoprazol, they had discovered changes in dogs' blood vessels, which are called vasculites. That meant it would be impossible to test picoprazol on humans. The news came as a complete shock to the project group and our research management. Once again we had been stopped just when we thought success was near, because of toxic effects.

At a project site visit at Hässle in 1978 the Group's Research Director and the board's scientific council went through all our projects. Through visits to our laboratories and discussions with researchers on different projects, they tried to develop a feeling how we carried out our work.

By that time I had, after twenty-four years, left my job as research director, but I was still part of the company management which was

ultimately responsible for research and development. I had been succeeded as research director by Karl Olof Borg.

When the Group's toxicologist, Torbjörn Malmfors presented the report on vasculites in dogs, everyone agreed we couldn't continue to
work with picoprazol, but what was worse was the renewed demand
that we should end the project. The attitude was that twelve years of
work had only created substances that could damage the body. Now
the end had come.

The Group's research director was unshakeable. We wouldn't continue to sacrifice time and money, he said firmly, on this project. He
was supported by two of the professors on the council. The Group's
new president Ulf Widengren was also very sceptical.

I made a last attempt. My strongest argument was that we had, so
far, always succeeded in finding scientific explanations for the problems that had confronted us. We had found new ways to go on when
our earlier efforts had led to compounds that could damage the thyroid and the immune system. There was a great probability that we
would succeed once again this time.

There were long discussions about what these vasculites really
meant. One theory was that the immune systems of the dogs were in
some way damaged by the picoprazol so that these mysterious injuries appeared in the blood vessels.

When the discussions ended, everyone seemed to be in agreement
with the recommendation that we terminate the project.

But while the discussion was going on, Björn Folkow had been
reading the toxicity report. Suddenly he burst out:

"Wait a minute! It says here that one dog in the control group also
had vasculites. That dog didn't receive any picoprazol and healthy
dogs aren't affected that way. There must be something wrong with
this study. We have to investigate this further before we can decide
what to do about the project."

Yet again the project had a new lease on life.

The Dog Fabian's Puppies

The task of solving the problem of the vasculites fell on a newly employed immunologist at Astra's safety laboratory, Vera Stejskal. Du-

188

ring the following year she carried out an impressive scientific detective hunt. Her key discovery was that the mysterious changes in the blood vessels only occurred in the offspring of a dog named Fabian.

Six of Fabian's seven puppies had been in the group that received picoprazol and another substance with a similar structure. All had developed vasculites. The remaining puppy had been in the control group and had not received any drugs. That dog also had vasculites. That was what saved the project.

Vera Stejskal discovered that the vasculites had appeared after the dogs were wormed. Probably Fabian's offspring suffered from a genetically damaged immune system. When the worms in the dogs' intestines were killed, this probably produced antibodies which apparently caused the damage to the blood vessels. When a new toxicity study was carried out on other dogs, there were no vasculites or other harmful effects.

Picoprazol had the effect we were aiming at and no damage had been observed in the new safety tests. We could now test its effect as an acid secretion inhibitor on humans.

An application for permission to carry out tests of picoprazol on human subjects was turned in to the Swedish Social Welfare Board and the ethical committee in May, 1979.

Gunnar Ekenved at Hässle's medical department carried out the studies on healthy human subjects together with Lars Olbe. For the first time in the project's history we could demonstrate that a substance we'd produced had the desired effect on acid secretion.

Simon Rune, medical director at a Danish hospital, heard about picoprazol. He asked for a sample so he could test the drug on patients with the severe illness, Zollinger-Ellison syndrome. These patients had gastrin-producing cancer tumours. The gastrin caused an abnormally high production of hydrochloric acid, which ate away at the stomach lining. The patients had the symptoms of ulcers. The doctor had tried all available medicines, but nothing had helped the worst sufferers, not even large doses of the new medicine Tagamet.

When he tried picoprazol on a patient, acid production sharply declined along with the pain after a dose of just 60 milligrams. Dr. Rune was impressed with the effects and reported on it to a medical congress.

We were now able to go on to clinical tests of picoprazol, and possibly to apply for registration as a finished drug.

There was, however, always a risk that someone at the approving authority would not accept our explanation for the vasculites in the dogs. For that reason, we were doubtful about continuing to concentrate on picoprazol.

During the forty years that I worked with drug research, I have several times been surprised at the ease with which a promising project can be killed off. To a certain extent, this may be because of a halfway application of the scientific method.

In research, positive results that indicate that a trial substance might be a useful medicine must always be confirmed with independent studies, before you dare believe in the results. But the converse is often forgotten. As soon as there is a negative discovery, such as the damage to the dogs' blood vessels, there is a tendency to accept these findings as conclusive. But you should be as sceptical to negative discoveries as to positive. They should also be confirmed with new studies, especially in cases that are crucial to the survival of an important project.

Thanks to the support we received from our consultants at the University of Gothenburg, and the independence we had won for ourselves within the Group, this project survived as did the projects which gave the Group the heart medicines alprenolol and metoprolol. It is hardly likely that any of these projects would have survived had Astra's research and development been more centrally controlled. Thanks to the decentralized research and product development that Arne Wegerfelt contributed to and supported, high risk projects could be initiated and carried through to the development of new products.

A Unique Medicine is Created

During the period that the new safety tests were being carried out with picoprazol, our chemists and pharmacologists continued to work in the hope of finding even better substances. The chemists systematically placed new groups of atoms in different parts of the basic molecular structure. They discovered that substances became more effective at inhibiting acid secretion if they were made more alkaline, by introducing groups into the ring that contained nitrogen. The idea was that the more alkaline these substances were, the more effective they

190

would be in seeking out the acid environment of the parietal cells of the stomach.

In a similar way, our researchers investigated how different atomic groups in other parts of the basic molecular structure improved the substances' biological characteristics.

In 1978-1979 we developed a group of ten compounds which were more effective acid secretion inhibitors than any previously tested and at the same time seemed to be completely non-toxic.

There were many factors to take into consideration when we had to choose one of these compounds for clinical tests for the final medicine. Not least stability and the ability to produce the substance in big quantities. The chosen substance also had to have the characteristics to make it possible to produce it in a suitable form. For the patients' convenience we wanted to be able to make tablets or capsules that only needed to be taken once a day.

For several reasons, we chose the compound H168/68. It was first synthesized on January 4, 1979, and was given the name omeprazol. It was approved for use in Sweden in February, 1988 under the brand name Losec. In the United States, the drug is marketed by Merck under the brand name Prilosec.

Chemist, Ylva Örtengren described how the name 168/68 was arrived at in an interview in the staff newsletter "Hässle-nytt" in 1990:

"I remember how our group head at the time, Ulf Junggren, jokingly told me to give this one a good number because he really believed in it. My journal was number 168. I was on page 22 and should have written the last step in the synthesis for the compound that became omeprazol on page 23. But when Ulf made that comment, I took him at his word and leafed forward to page 68. That's how it got the name 168/68."

Obviously, she didn't think H168/23 was a good enough name for a compound that was expected to be an valuable medicine.

More than 800 new substances had been developed and tested on animals. Including the intermediate products used to make a finished compound, that means several thousand new chemical compounds were made in the course of the project.

Chemists Peder Berntsson, Ulf Junggren, and their colleagues had carried out an impressive ten year effort, where together with pharmacologist Sven-Erik Sjöstrand, they methodically carried the project to its completion. A whole new group of chemical compounds had been developed and patented. A medicine with a unique ability to inhibit the secretion of hydrochloric acid in the stomach had been created. Most interesting, from a scientific point of view, is that a new biological mechanism was discovered.

How that discovery was made is an interesting story in itself.

The University of Uppsala's 500th Anniversary

For that we have to go back to 1977 when Sweden's oldest college, the University of Uppsala, celebrated its 500th anniversary. As part of the celebrations, a different international scientific symposium was held in Uppsala every month during the year.

The symposium in July was called "Gastric Ion Transport". It concerned the mechanisms that regulate the secretion of gastric juices. The participants from Hässle's project group were our consultant Lars Olbe, pharmacologists, Sven-Erik Sjögren and Gunhild Sundell, and biochemist, Erik Fellenius. Another participant was histologist, Herbert Helander, a Hässle consultant who was later employed by the company.

Professor Georg Sachs and his colleagues from the United States presented studies which immediately caught the attention of the Hässle group. A new enzyme called hydrogen-potassium-ATPase (hydrogen-potassium-adenosine triphosphatase) had been discovered in the stomach's parietal cells. Sachs and his colleagues reported that they had investigated some twenty other organs in rats. Only in the thyroid gland had they found the same or what was possibly a similar enzyme.

In her report from the Uppsala symposium, Gunhild Sundell wrote:

"Sachs' talk was immediately followed by the lunch break, when we managed to stand in the food line together with Sachs and his colleague Saccomani. We asked if they hadn't possibly 'forgotten' some other organ with a positive reaction? Had they investigated the thymus? Yes, they had actually, and had gotten a positive reaction, but the interpretation of this discovery had been so uncertain that they hadn't taken it up in the lecture.

"When they discovered that the only reactions to our substances (the benzimidazols) had been in the stomach's acid producing section, and in some cases the thyroid and the thymus, a lively discussion broke out. This continued during dinners, in corridors and during a tennis match. These discussions were the beginning of a real interest from Sach's, and the start of a fine collaboration."

Gundhild Sundell's report gives a picture of how researchers can be stimulated by an important discovery and how that discovery can be complemented by the findings of other researchers.

The interesting factor was that our compound, H83/69 had a (desired) effect on acid secretion, but also had (undesired) effects on the thyroid and the thymus. This indicated that the same, or a very similar, enzyme system existed in all three organs. As mentioned earlier, we were successful in changing the chemical structure of the compound to remove the effects on the thyroid and the thymus. This indicated that the enzyme in the parietal cells differed from the enzyme in the other two organs. By developing a drug that only affected one enzyme in one single organ, the risk of side effects in other organs was diminished. There was reason to believe that the drug would not affect any other organ than the stomach's parietal cells.

Because of this contact, we understood the mechanism behind our new acid secretion compounds and gained confidence that the risk of undesired side effects was very slight. An association between Georg Sachs and Hässle lasting many years began thanks to the contacts made at the celebrations of the University of Uppsala's 500th anniversary.

Research conducted over a period of several years gradually revealed the details of the mechanism behind omeprazol. Arne Brändström's contributions attracted international attention as they clarified the physical-chemical mechanisms involved when omeprazol intervenes in acid secretion. For scientific contributions that included this work, Arne was rewarded with the Gold Medal of the Swedish Academy of Engineering Science in 1988.

Here is an outline of the mechanism behind omeprazol's acid secretion inhibiting effect:

In the stomach lining, which is about one millimetre thick, there are glands which contain the cells which produce hydrochloric acid. These cells are called parietal cells. Altogether there are around one billion of them in the stomach.

Working like a kind of pump within these acid producing cells is

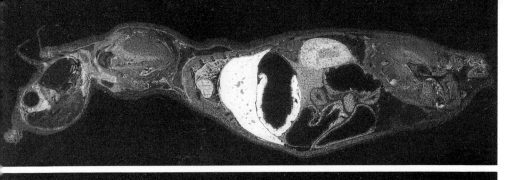

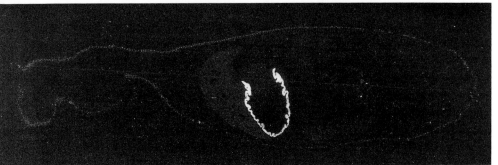

These photographs, taken at ASTRA's high security laboratory, show the spread of radioactive Losec in a mouse's body. One minute after the drug was intravenously administered, it had spread throughout the vascular system. The lower picture was taken 16 hours later and shows that the Losec is now only present in the oxygen producing cells of the stomach. *Hässle's archives.*

an enzyme which transports hydrogen ions to the acid cavity in the parietal cell where the hydrochloric acid is made. That enzyme is hydrogen-potassium-ATPase. The drug omeprazol has the remarkable characteristic of not having any known effect on any organ other than the stomach's parietal cells. Omeprazol does not remain, and cannot be found, in any other organ. This has been shown by Astra's safety laboratory using autoradiography, where omeprazol was marked with a radioactive atom. The path of the omeprazol through the blood in a mouse could be followed using X-ray pictures. A few minutes after an injection, the drug was in all the blood vessels. After a few hours, the omeprazol could be found only in the stomach lining, and there only in the parietal cells. The omeprazol could be seen as white spots in the stomach in the X-ray pictures. The rest of the mouse was black, indicating the absence of the drug.

Omeprazol as such has no other effect, even in the parietal cells. As soon as it arrives in the acidic cavity of the cell where the hydrochloric acid is produced, the omeprazol is converted within a few seconds to another chemical compound. It is this compound which combines with the enzyme hydrogen-potassium-ATPase to block the so-called proton pump. No more hydrochloric acid is produced. Omeprazol's effect can be described as an inhibitor of the proton pump within the parietal cells.

Along with Arne Brändström and Karl Olof Borg, pharmacologist, Enar Carlsson also investigated omeprazol's working mechanism. Enar Carlsson was the project manager responsible for the omeprazol project from 1981. Other researchers who made meaningful contributions to this complicated scientific work were biochemists, Erik Fellenius, Björn Wallmark and Hillevi Mattson, and histolgist, Herbert Helander.

A Difficult Drug to Handle

When chemists create a new substance, there is a long road left before a useful medicine is produced.

As far as omeprazol was concerned, it turned out that this substance was uncommonly difficult to work with. Omeprazol was sensitive to light, water and heat, and broke down on exposure to any of these. It couldn't be made into tablets and when we tried to use it in capsules, the omeprazol was immediately destroyed by the hydrochloric acid in the stomach.

Our pharmacists were forced to develop completely new methods to make the finished medicine. They produced small grains with protective membranes that could withstand exposure to the stomach's hydrochloric acid. To accomplish this, completely new machines and production techniques had to be developed.

When capsules, each with hundreds of grains inside, are dissolved in the stomach, the grains spread out. The membrane around each grain protect the omeprazol from the stomach's hydrochloric acid. The membranes finally dissolve when the grains arrive at the duodenum. The omeprazol is absorbed through the wall of the intestine and is transported via the blood to the stomach's parietal cells.

The Most Serious Setback was a False Alarm

Beginning in 1981, comprehensive clinical tests were carried out in a large number of countries. They were co-ordinated and managed by Gunnar Ekenved. He had been involved in the field of ulcer medicines since the first product development and research. The clinical test program was planned together with Lennar Sölvell and Anders Walan, who were responsible for peptic ulcer medicines within Hässle's Medical Division.

Nowadays, clinical tests are the most expensive part of a research project. For several years during the 80's, our annual budget for these tests was 10 to 12 million dollars.

All tests from the hospitals where omeprazol was tried showed positive results. Everything seemed very good. We prepared our registration applications to the authorities in different countries.

In May 1984 I was in Bangalore, India, where I was working to build up a center for biotechnology and molecular biological research. A telex arrived from Hässle.

A number of cancer-like tumours had been found in rats that had been given omeprazol. The discovery had come at the end of a two year cancer study in the United States. All clinical trials had been stopped.

This naturally came as a shock to those of us who had struggled with the project for so many years and were now so sure we were near our goal. From what I later heard, for the first two weeks after the news, the researchers were close to giving up. It was the fifth time the project had been threatened with termination or suspension. But this was the most serious setback during the project's entire twenty-two year history.

Under the direction of my successor Karl Olof Borg, a group was organized to find a scientific explanation for these tumours in rats.

Pathologist Niilo Havu made an important contribution when he succeeded in demonstrating that these tumours had nothing to do with cancer. In a letter to me in March 1991 he explained:

"I went to the Hazleton Laboratories in the United States to witness what we thought was the end of omeprazol, but I discovered that they had wrongly diagnosed carcinoides. At first Hazleton's pathologists all agreed that they had found cancer and none accepted my explanation.

"Using silver dyes I succeeded in convincing the responsible pathologist that they had discovered carcinoides and not cancer. Using special dyes we could prove that the ECL cells were involved. The connection between gastrin and ECL cells was known. On June 6, 1984 the so-called Gastrin Hypothesis was presented to the Swedish Social Welfare Board's Drug Division in Uppsala. My part was in demonstrating the morphology of ECL cells in young and old rats. The drug division accepted the explanation that cancer was not involved."

Consequently it was completely established that the changes observed in rat stomach linings had nothing to do with cancer. Furthermore, long term studies on mice and dogs had not revealed any changes resembling those that had been observed in rats.

Enar Carlsson, who for ten years had made important contributions to our beta-blocker project, had in a short time found himself involved in completely new problems in the acid secretion project. After Karl Olof Borg left Hässle, Enar Carlsson, as Director of Research, was responsible for ulcer medicines. Together with Lennart Sölvell, who was attached to the project as medical advisor, and in co-operation with Herbert Helander, Enar Carlsson succeeded in less than a year to find an explanation for how such changes could occur in rats.

The clinical tests could be resumed in the late Fall of 1985.

We had already observed in our first unsuccessful tests in the late 60's that rats react differently to acid secretion inhibitors than do humans and other animals. The compounds that had a good effect on rats had no effect on dogs or humans. Lars Olbe had already told us that rats react differently to the hormone, gastrin.

For several years, research continued in order to explain the changes that had been observed in rats. It was discovered that these ECL cells were created no matter what means were used to reduce acid secretion. Even when the part of the rats' stomachs where the acid was produced was surgically removed, the rats reacted by producing large quantities of gastrin creating these changes. It could be convincingly demonstrated that the changes were not due to the drug omeprazol.

By the time the application for the registration of omeprazol, under the name Losec, was filed, 9,000 patients in some forty countries had participated in the clinical trials program. The name Losec was derived from "Low Secretion".

197

The results of the clinical trials were very positive. We had been able to prove above all that treatment with 20-40 milligrams a day of omeprazol greatly reduced hydrochloric acid secretion in humans for twenty-four hours, unlike earlier ulcer medicines such as the H2 blockers.

It was important to be able to show that a slight acid secretion remained during treatment with the recommended doses of omeprazol. Because the acid secretion did not completely disappear, the release of gastrin increased only moderately.

No signs of harmful effects have been observed in long term studies where patients have used omeprazol for several years.

The research that was carried out for a number of years after 1984, and the results of the comprehensive clinical trials program, convinced the responsible authorities in all the countries where applications for registration were filed that omeprazol is an effective and safe drug. Omeprazol is now registered in more than eighty countries, including the United States and Japan.

The experience of all these clinical tests as well as omeprazol's first seven years on the market is that a dose as low as 20 milligrams administered once a day gives rapid pain relief. Ulcers in the oesophagus, stomach and duodenum heal within two weeks in 80 percent of all cases which have received 20 milligrams a day. The previously most used ulcer medicines, the H2 blockers cimetidin and ranitidin, require four weeks to reach approximately the same result. After four weeks treatment with 20 milligrams of omeprazol per day, more than 90 percent of patients are free of their suffering.

After twenty-two years of work in a project that included 150 researchers and technicians, at a total cost in 1988 monetary value of USD 170 million, a unique medicine had been created. I agree completely with what Hässle's Information Director Erik Holm wrote in the publication "Aktuellt om Hässle 1989" ("The Latest from Hässle 1989"):

"With the introduction of Losec, Hässle has written a paragraph of medical history as the creator of a completely new class of drugs. A physician at the Akademiska Hospital in Uppsala wrote in an article:

"'With omeprazol you can reassure your ulcer patient that he or she is receiving the most effective relief from there symptoms that science knows, and healing at a frequency and rapidity that is today unexcelled.'"

198

The Causes of Set-Backs and Successes

None of the six projects which were started at Hässle in 1959 and 1960 resulted in a useful medicine being created. There were several reasons.

We lacked experience in biological-chemical research. We were highly competent in chemistry, but we lacked both the resources and the competence in pharmacology and other biological sciences.

The way we chose to work was traditional at that time in the pharmaceutical industry. You synthesized a large number of compounds, which were tested using known pharmacological methods in the hope of finding a substance which could be refined into something worth testing on people. In most cases, pharmaceutical researchers were forced to produce thousands of compounds before they found a useful drug. We lacked such resources.

The new direction we were given by Arvid Carlsson in May, 1961 was the beginning of a new approach for us. He advised us to work with new biological principles. For the heart medicine project, he recommended that we concentrate on developing beta-blockers, which led us to alprenolol and metoprolol.

Even if this guidance was decisive, it was nevertheless essential that a number of other conditions be met in order for the project to lead to better medicines. In the long run, it is only products that can be documented as improvements over those already on the market which are likely to survive international competition.

To summarize my experience, I would like to name the following preconditions as the most important for a research and development organization to create these kind of products:

1. A high degree of competence is a precondition for the creation of products based on patent-protected innovations. We built up and developed our competence through a close collaboration with university researchers, primarily at the Pharmaceutical Faculty at the University of Uppsala, and the Medical Faculty at the University of Gothenburg. Broad qualifications are required, particularly within pharmaceutical research. A precondition for success is that you create a constructive interplay between researchers from different scientific disciplines.

2. A company's long term goals are of major importance in attracting and keeping qualified personnel in all areas. Hässle's goals from the beginning of 1972 were decisive for our future development.
Our long term goal was to create medicines which would contribute to the development of pharmaco-therapy. It meant that the drugs would be better than the medicines already available to physicians. This would have to be demonstrated by proper documentation.

3. A climate of innovation is decisive for creativity and productivity in a research and development organization. The company management and project managers' will and ability to motivate, stimulate and reward innovators are important factors. Positive leadership at all levels in the company is essential for the proper climate. A sense of security in a research and development organization is necessary if scientists and technicians are willing to risk devoting themselves to difficult, apparently impossible, projects. If this security is missing, there's a risk the projects that are pursued will lead to "me too" products, that is, products that are variations on other companies' successful innovations. One way that this security is created is when the personnel know the project manager will take responsibility should a project fail.

4. The company's personnel must also be aware of the external insecurity in the company's struggle to survive and develop against hard international competition.

5. Available resources must be in reasonable relation to the complexity and number of projects being carried out. One thing is clear, however, large resources in themselves are no guarantee for success. When

200

a research and development organization is growing, there is always a risk that bureaucracy and inflexible rules will reduce personal initiative and the fighting spirit that is a prerequisite for creativity.

6. Decentralizing into smaller research and development organizations, each with a relatively large degree of freedom, has been one of the most important prerequisites for developing products that have been the foundation of Astra's international success.

7. More important than expanding resources, is the will to set priorities and the ability to concentrate resources on those projects. Also important for the climate of a research and development organization is how management treats researchers and technicians who are enthusiastically working on projects given low priority or which have to be discontinued. A flexible research and development organization is a precondition for being able to concentrate resources on priority projects.

8. The choice of the right project managers for the different development phases of a project can be of decisive importance for success. In the project that led to omeprazol, project managers were changed four times. When changing project managers, it is crucial that the research director insures that continuity is maintained.

9. The managers' will and ability to deal with conflicts is of greater importance than most project managers seem to realize. Conflicts can be constructive and can carry a project forward. It rests on the manager to deal with them in the right way.

10. The willingness of company management, research directors and project managers to listen to criticism is a prerequisite for competence and understanding under control. The leader who surrounds himself with 'yes men' will sooner or later lose the respect and confidence of his colleagues.

The list of prerequisites for success can be made longer. People can have varying opinions about which of these ten factors is the most important. But of one thing I am convinced: if my colleagues within all areas at Hässle's research and development organization had not had a strong desire to create worthwhile medicines and indomitable will to continue despite difficulties, then this relatively small group would never have succeeded in creating metoprolol, felodipin and omeprazol, the three products that have been of the greatest importance for Astra, and can be expected to remain so during the rest of the decade.

Everyday Heroes

When you talk about milestones on the way, many of the everyday "heroes" unfortunately remain in the background. Not least this includes colleagues at departments which haven't directly participated in the process of innovation. I'm thinking here, for example, of the important contributions made by colleagues at the analysis laboratories. Their creativity resulted in the development of highly complicated new methods. Through their fine work, hundreds of thousands of analyses have been carried out.

Another example is the statisticians who, through processing and studying data, have been able to throw light upon the characteristics of the drugs under study.

Those who have worked on registration applications, which encompassed hundreds of loose-leaf notebooks filled with documents, have often, during the final stages of a project, been forced to work overtime night after night. More colleagues deserve to be mentioned as well.

For me it has been a great privilege to be part of this team of capable and enthusiastic people. Naturally the successes, when we reached our goals, have been wonderful experiences. The common struggle against set-backs and apparently impossible difficulties provided a joy which I remember with gratitude.

The innovations of the researchers and technicians didn't get the appreciation they deserved until they were successfully marketed against international competition. Astra's skill and resources for the production and international marketing of quality drugs made it possible for Hässle's innovations to become billion dollar products.

V. An Attempt at Some Perspective

The last few decades have seen fascinating developments within the world of medicine. Those who weren't involved during this period must find it difficult to understand how doctors' abilities to cure illness and relieve pain have been transformed. Scientific discoveries, clinical experience and the creation of new medicines have made these developments possible.

Fifty Years of Progress

In the industrialized countries, with their high standard of living, polio has, for example, been eliminated. A very effective vaccine, first developed by Jonas Salk, protects against this once feared paralyzer of children.

There's no longer a threat of dying from pneumonia, blood poisoning or a ruptured appendix. Penicillin and other antibiotics, developed in the 40's and 50's, have given doctors the ability to cure most infectious diseases.

Before 1960 there was no way to effectively treat patients suffering from severe depression or schizophrenia. Thanks to the drugs created by the major pharmaceutical companies, many patients have been able to leave mental hospitals.

During the Second World War there was nothing to give patients with high blood pressure. Today, there are several drugs which use differing mechanisms to normalize high blood pressure. Side effects

Farewell Symposium at Hässle in March, 1983.
From the left: Arvid Carlsson, Sven-Arne Nordlindh, Ivan Östholm, Leif Hallberg, Göran Schill, Lars Werkö and Lars Olbe.

are, as a rule, small, compared to the "side effects" of untreated high blood pressure.

In the 40's and far into the 50's, after a heart attack the treatment was six weeks in bed, followed by a rest period of three to six months in which patients were not allowed to return to work or other duties. Clinical research has led the way to new methods of treatment. The rehabilitation of heart attack patients now often begins after only one or two weeks in bed. Thanks to new drugs that protect the heart from different forms of physical and emotional stress, these patients can lead active lives much longer than before. The risk of suddenly dying after a heart attack has been greatly reduced.

During the 70's and 80's, drugs were created that so effectively block acidic secretions from stomach ulcers that these can heal in

Vision for the Year 2000

This drawing shows the future Astra Hässle, as the company has been called since July 1991. The white buildings existed in 1991. The dark buildings are to be built before the year 2,000.

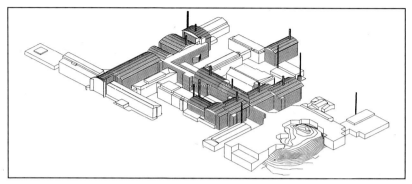

During the 1990's the company estimates that it will spend more than USD 100 million on construction and laboratory equipment. This investment shows strong belief in the company's future from the Astra board and Group President, Håkan Mogren. Astra Hässle's President, Anders Vedin, says: "It is our successful research over the years and a strong belief in our current research projects that lie behind this investment."

Drawing: Wingårdh & Wingårdh

two to four weeks. The need to operate on bleeding ulcers has been drastically reduced.

Thanks to new methods of treatment, asthma patients today have completely new opportunities for active lives than they did just a few decades ago.

Some forms of cancer can be cured today. Others can be treated with surgical operations, radiation treatment or drugs, so that cancer patients can live for several more years. Better means of early diagnosis and new methods of treatment have given encouraging results, but much remains to be done.

The list of doctors' possibilities to help their patients with modern medicines grows longer and longer. There is good reason to agree with Nobel laureate, Ernst Chain, who wrote: "For my part, I believe that medicines are one of the blessings of our age, perhaps the greatest of them all".

"The Drugs of the Future?

Looking into to the next century, I believe there is hope for important progress in all of these areas. Even if most new drugs continue to come from major multi-national companies, the Swedish pharmaceutical industry can still make important contributions to the medicine treasure chest of the future.

One thing is clear: only when knowledge from basic research and competence within a research and development organization coincide with medical needs is there a reason to start projects aimed at developing new medicines. Considering the current state of research, and the fact that it takes ten to fifteen years or more to develop a new medicine from idea to documented product, we can expect progress in several areas.

When will we solve the riddle of cancer? When will we have effective drugs to cure cancer? These questions are often put to researchers. Those who are in the front line of cancer research usually answer: There really isn't a cancer riddle any more. We have a good picture of why and how tumours appear. Partly because there are so many different forms of cancer, we'll probably never find a universal cure, but today, many cases of cancer can be cured and others can be treated, adding many years of active life. What we can hope to achieve in the next ten to fifteen years is to improve diagnostic methods, so that tumours can be spotted at a much earlier stage.

Thanks to new developments in bio-technology, we can expect to develop bio-sensors which make it possible to track down cancer.

Through genetic engineering and hybridoma technology, we ought to be able to create new agents to control cell toxins, cytostatica, so they can attack cancer cells in particular organs without hurting other parts of the body's tissues or organs. Important progress will probably also be made within immunology research. We can expect to develop new drugs to strengthen the body's own immunological defences, to kill cancer cells.

As far as reducing the suffering and the risk of death from cancer, it's important that people adopt healthier lifestyles and especially stop smoking.

As far as everyday illnesses are concerned, such as influenza and upper respiratory diseases, there is a major need for drugs that can strengthen resistance, but there's little chance that a vaccine or new drug can bring about major improvements in the near future.

Cures for rheumatic illnesses, muscular dystrophy and multiple sclerosis are high on the list of urgent medical needs. Here, as well, there is hope that new techniques in molecular biology will point to new kinds of treatment. Researchers working with genetic engineering have reported that they have succeeded in clarifying the chemical structure of the receptors on the muscle cells that are connected with the most common form of muscular dystrophy. Another research group has succeeded in animal experiments in introducing into damaged muscles the enzyme needed for transporting energy to the muscles. Hopefully, these discoveries will lead to medicines to repair damaged muscles.

The treatment of diabetes today is far from satisfactory, dependent as it is on insulin injections. Diabetes is a such a complicated disease, with a tendency to damage many different organs, that completely new methods of treatment are needed. Those who have been carrying out basic research have in recent years succeeded in clarifying mechanisms that contribute to our understanding of how diabetes arises. It is possible that these discoveries will lead to new medicines after the turn of the century.

There is a great need to develop medicines to prevent and treat osteoporoses, fragile bones, which is a great handicap, mainly for women, and which costs society a great deal. Because researchers have now perceived this need, we can expect that new methods of treatment will be forthcoming.

The ability of bio-technology to help researchers determine the exact chemical structure of receptors, receivers of signals in various organs, such as the heart, bronchi and the brain, ought to help carry research forward. We should expect new medicines with more specific effects on ailing organs for heart diseases such as severe arrhythmias, asthma, allergies and mental illnesses. When the receptors in different organs can be determined, it will be easier to "design" drugs for illnesses in these organs with less risk of undesirable side effects in other organs.

By the year 2,000, researchers should have completely charted the structure of the human genetic code. When this is accomplished, we will be able to understand more about the 4,000 diseases caused by genetic changes. In the future, gene therapy may be possible. "Healthy" genes can be introduced to replace the genetic bits that have caused a particular disease.

In all these advances, pharmaceutical research has played, and will continue to play, an important role. This isn't just the production of new medications. Another important side of this research is the creation of new molecules that can serve as tools for the investigation of the processes of life. The deeper understanding we can win thanks to such tools continues to open new perspectives and new directions for the combating of sickness and suffering.

VI. Challenges After the Year 2000

It was an inspired lecture in 1946 that instilled in me the desire to participate in the search for useful medicines. The chemist, Nils Löfgren described how he and a colleague had succeeded in developing the world's best local anaesthetic. With great insight he spoke of several years' struggle to overcome set-backs before the two scientists came up with the compound that became lidocain (marketed as Xylocain®).

In his speech, Löfgren succeeded in conveying a feeling for the joy of the researchers felt when they achieved their goal: a medicine that was better than all others on the market.

This hope to participate in the discovery of medicines to satisfy medical needs have been fulfilled thanks to the innovations of Hässle's scientists and technicians in collaboration with colleagues at Swedish universities.

If you look back fifty years to when this story began, you find unimaginable progress in the world of medicine. Back then, around 1940, there was an incredible lack of effective medicines that today's young reader can hardly imagine. For the few medicines that did exist, science was still in the dark about how they worked and what doses should be used. During the half century since then we have gone from folklore and guesswork to true understanding. Effective, well-documented medicines have been developed to an extent that no one could have foreseen in the 1940's.

What can we hope for in the future? What are the possibilities that in fifty years time we will be able to treat illnesses for which there are no cures today?

In all probability, we can expect that people in the coming decades will expect an improved quality of life. After industrial society's concentration on higher economic and material standards, interest will more and more be directed towards questions concerning the inner and outer environment. It is against this perspective that one should see the great challenges that await researchers.

To put right environmental destruction and prevent further abuse of the earth's limited resources, is a gigantic task which falls outside my competence to discuss. But one thing ought to be certain: it is only through biological and chemical research that these problems can be solved.

Where human health is concerned, what I call the inner environment, there are urgent challenges which certainly should stimulate scientists to undertake daring and difficult projects.

Without putting them in any order of importance, I would like to point out a few urgent needs which may become the challenges confronted by the researchers of tomorrow.

Age-Related Sicknesses

Young people, who see how so many of the elderly are forced to live undignified lives handicapped by age-related diseases, must surely realize how important it is to find ways to prevent arteriosclerosis and its complications. Senile dementia, Alzheimer's disease, memory loss and other damage caused by destructive changes in the central nervous system are some of the most pressing targets for future research. The 90's have been called the Decade of the Brain in the United States. This has focused the interest of researchers on these problems and at the same time underlined the new opportunities made possible by recent discoveries.

By finding drugs that increase blood circulation in the brain, and other drugs that increase the level of the signal substances, we can probably improve the functioning of the brain. In a few decades, it may be possible to transplant healthy brain tissue which could help repair damaged tissue.

Abuse

The problems of alcohol and narcotics abuse have become so great that they are almost impossible to deal with. For those who want to end their addiction, but cannot because of withdrawal symptoms and the continued craving to feed their habit, it is vital that we find medicines to counteract withdrawal symptoms and reduce the desire for the drug, the two greatest causes of relapse. Recent research into the brain's signal substances has begun to give insights into the mechanisms that lie behind the craving and suggest possible treatment.

A much more difficult problem lies in what can be given to those who don't want to end their abuse of intoxicants. It is probably impossible to develop an ideal drug to satisfy the craving for intoxication. There will always be some negative effects in any drug. The key to helping these people is therefore outside the area of pharmaceutical research. Politicians, teachers and other social leaders will have to discover new ways to help people find meaningful lives where they are no longer tempted to turn to narcotics and other intoxicants.

The Developing Countries and Genetic Engineering

The youth of the 90's and the future will, more than previous generations, come into contact with people in the Third World. While travelling in developing countries they will see the enormous problems facing the Third World. The need to help the developing countries find medicines for the treatment of tropical diseases is becoming more and more acute. During the 80's when I was building up Astra's center for bio-technical research in India, I saw for myself the extent of the problem of tropical diseases. Large resources are already being devoted to cure and prevent malaria. The new fields of bio-technology and genetic engineering should open new paths to the solution of these problems.

In conversations with biochemists in Sweden and at the Indian research center I now understand of how researchers are studying thousands of diseases caused by genetic mutations. There is hope that, in the future, we will be able to insert "healthy" genes to replace the genetic bits that cause a particular disease. We will be able to reduce human suffering to a degree that can't be imagined today.

Cancer

Everyone is waiting for the researchers to find better ways to discover cancer at an early stage and cure this terrible disease. New discoveries in molecular biology and immunological research will undoubtedly open new paths in cancer research. Here, just as in viral research on AIDS, great problems await committed researchers.

Side Effects

One pressing task for pharmaceutical research is to further reduce the risk of side effects. The safety tests now carried out undoubtedly prevent serious side effects. It is, however, urgent that we find new methods to establish the risk for rare and illusive side effects, such as blood changes and allergic skin reactions, which for immunological reasons can sometimes be fatal. With the discoveries that are now being made within immunological research, we can expect that methods to uncover such side effects will be developed. For the same reason we can look forward to interesting developments within the field of immunologically-based illnesses such as rheumatoid arthritis.

The Dream is Fulfilled

During the 40's, when I dreamed of taking part in the quest for new medicines, I never suspected that we would succeed in creating drugs that would help millions of patients all over the world to live healthier lives.

Despite tough international competition, several of the Astra Group's projects succeeded in creating products that are among the most important medicines in the world. Two of these drugs have been in the "global top ten". This is quite remarkable considering that the Swedish pharmaceutical industry, taken as a whole, has at its disposal

212

only one and a half percent of the world's total resources for pharmaceutical research and product development. One of the reasons is probably the high standard of biological and clinical research in Sweden and the companies' ability to utilize this national resource.

Co-operation is Important

One of this book's most important messages is the value of close collaboration between industry's research and development departments and university researchers. The close collaboration that Hässle built up, especially with the Medical Faculty at the University of Gothenburg and the Pharmaceutical Faculty at the University of Uppsala, has been described abroad as "A Swedish Model".

The research and development investments of the pharmaceutical industry in countries such as Britain, Japan, Switzerland, Germany and the United States would undoubtedly pay more dividends if they succeeded in establishing better contact with university researchers following our "Swedish model". But my contacts with companies in those countries indicates that they have difficulty building trusting and open relations with university departments.

The position of adjutant professor which was introduced into Swedish universities in 1973 was an important step in easing collaboration between industry and academia. Perhaps the next step would be some kind of "job rotation", so that it would be natural to move back and forth between university and industry. We will probably discover that the boundary between basic research at the university and industry's exploratory and goal-oriented research will blur. That's one reason why it should be easier for university researchers to move to industry in the future.

When I wrote down the first project notes in May, 1954, for what was to become the first section of this book, I used an old-fashioned fountain pen in Hässle's primitively equipped laboratories. As I write these final lines in the book's last chapter, I'm using a laptop computer. This might be as good an illustration as any of what has happened during the period I have tried to portray. So what do I want to say?

Dare to Take Challenges!

To patients reading about "their medicine", how it was created and works, I would like to underline the great advances these new medicines have meant for healthcare and for physicians' ability to effectively treat disease. Considering the great resources that are now being devoted to pharmaceutical research and to the new knowledge that is being gained every year, patients have every reason to look forward to the development of new medicines to meet more of the world's remaining medical challenges.

To pharmaceutical researchers in industry and to researchers and specialists at government agencies, I would like to direct a challenge to find ways to shorten the time from the discovery of a new drug to the approval for its use, at the same time maintaining high safety standards.

Just as chemist Nils Löfgren inspired in me a desire to join in the quest for new and better medicines, I hope that the researchers of today and tomorrow are motivated to take on the many challenges that remain. Perhaps the story of our successes can in some way stimulate researchers and technicians. If anyone hesitates in taking on really difficult challenges, because they think "it was easier and better before", they are mistaken. Our accumulated understanding of biomedicine is so much more now than when we started the projects covered in this book that the chances of succeeding are, and will become, even better.

In order to succeed, what is needed most is the continued growth of professional competence in close collaboration with basic research and the "fighting spirit" that the researchers in this book demonstrated over and over again when they overcame apparently impossible obstacles. The future, with the growing demands that will be placed on leaders, researchers and technicians, lies in the hands of the new generation.

Trade marks for drugs discovered by projects in this book.

Generic name	Trade marks
Alprenolol	Aptin.
Felodipin	Plendil, Flodil, Modip, Splendil.
Metoprolol	Seloken, Seloken ZOC, Selo-Zok, Beloc, Beloc ZOK, Betaloc, Betaloc ZOK, Betaloc ZR, Lopressor. Toprol-XL.
Omeprazol	Losec, Antra, Gastroloc, Mopral, Mepral, Omepral, Omeprazen, Prilosec.